About Pfeiffer

Pfeiffer serves the professional developme   raining and human
resource practitioners and gives them pr   .eliver proven ideas
and solutions from experts in HR development and HR management, and we offer effective and
customizable tools to improve workplace performance. From novice to seasoned professional,
Pfeiffer is the source you can trust to make yourself and your organization more successful.

Essential Knowledge Pfeiffer produces insightful, practical, and comprehensive
materials on topics that matter the most to training and HR professionals. Our Essential Knowledge
resources translate the expertise of seasoned professionals into practical, how-to guidance on
critical workplace issues and problems. These resources are supported by case studies, worksheets,
and job aids and are frequently supplemented with CD-ROMs, websites, and other means of
making the content easier to read, understand, and use.

Essential Tools Pfeiffer's Essential Tools resources save time and expense by offering
proven, ready-to-use materials—including exercises, activities, games, instruments, and assessments—for use during a training or-team-learning event. These resources are frequently offered
in looseleaf or CD-ROM format to facilitate copying and customization of the material.

Pfeiffer also recognizes the remarkable power of new technologies in expanding the reach and
effectiveness of training. While e-hype has often created whizbang solutions in search of a problem, we are dedicated to bringing convenience and enhancements to proven training solutions.
All our e-tools comply with rigorous functionality standards. The most appropriate technology
wrapped around essential content yields the perfect solution for today's on-the-go trainers and
human resource professionals.

Pfeiffer
www.pfeiffer.com

Essential resources for training and HR professionals

An Instructor's Manual for *Rapid Training Development: Developing Training Courses Fast and Right* is available FREE online. The Manual provides instruction in using *Rapid Training Development* as a basis for teaching courses in instructional design or development techniques. It also offers activities and exercises which might be used in a classroom setting in conjunction with the book.

If you would like to download and print a copy of the Instructor's Manual, please visit **www.wiley.com/college/piskurich**

Rapid Training Development

Developing Training Courses Fast and Right

George M. Piskurich

Pfeiffer
A Wiley Imprint
www.pfeiffer.com

Published by Pfeiffer

An Imprint of Wiley

989 Market Street, San Francisco, CA 94103-1741 www.pfeiffer.com

For additional copies/bulk purchases of this book in the U.S. please contact 800-274-4434.

Pfeiffer books and products are available through most bookstores. To contact Pfeiffer directly call our Customer Care Department within the U.S. at 800-274-4434, outside the U.S. at 317-572-3985, fax 317-572-4002, or visit www.pfeiffer.com.

Pfeiffer also publishes its books in a variety of electronic formats. Some content that appears in print may not be available in electronic books.

Library of Congress Cataloging-in-Publication Data

Piskurich, George M.
    Rapid training development : developing training courses fast and right / George M. Piskurich.
        p.   cm.
    Includes bibliographical references and index.
    ISBN 978-0-470-39977-4 (pbk.)
        1. Instructional systems–Design.   I. Title.
    LB1028.38.P568   2009
    371.3–dc22

                                                                                2009001140

Acquiring Editor: Matthew Davis
Director of Development: Kathleen Dolan Davies
Production Editor: Dawn Kilgore

Editor: Rebecca Taff
Editorial Assistant: Michael Gilbart
Manufacturing Supervisor: Becky Morgan

Printed in the United States of America

Printing   10 9 8 7 6 5 4 3 2 1

Contents

Preface

The purpose of this volume is to pick up where *Rapid Instructional Design* left off by helping you to more efficiently and effectively develop training programs once you have completed, or sort of completed, the design phase of instructional systems design. This book does this by providing you with course development thoughts, hints, and shortcuts of a general nature that could be useful for almost any design and then continuing this approach with techniques that are specific to each major delivery process. Many of these thoughts, hints, and shortcuts are further illuminated by actual examples, checklists, and case studies.

The book is divided into chapters based on delivery systems to make it easier for you to find the information you need for the design you are developing and to create a certain synergy among the techniques as you can see how they work together in a singular design.

This doesn't mean that you won't find many of the rapid development techniques useful for deliveries other than the one they appear with; it was simply an easier way to structure the information without becoming too redundant.

After the first chapter, which is on general rapid development techniques that can be useful for a number of deliveries, the other chapters are focused on single delivery processes, starting with the most common, the classroom, and finishing with the most different, and possibly most overlooked, performance aids. In some cases the chapters not only consider rapid development techniques for the delivery system, but also how the system itself can be a rapid development shortcut for other types of deliveries. For example, synchronous e-learning is a delivery system unto itself, with any number of rapid development shortcuts, but by using it in lieu of some parts of an asynchronous e-learning package it becomes a rapid development technique for the asynchronous delivery. I hope this won't confuse the issue too much, as it is an important aspect of rapid development.

The last chapter looks at some delivery processes, such as mobile learning, that have not been around long enough to have a lot of rapid development shortcuts and some processes that aren't really considered delivery systems, but can certainly be rapid development shortcuts, such as knowledge management and reusable content objects.

For our colleagues in academia, this book can be used as a teaching tool, giving students a reference source for all of the major delivery systems and professors a single development text to teach from in any type of training- or learning-oriented class.

In the end it is the wise developer who chooses the right development techniques for his or her environment and personal skills, but I hope that this book can provide some other possibilities and help make that choosing a little easier.

Introduction: What Course Development Is and Is Not

*T*here is a singular disadvantage to training that probably outweighs all the other disadvantages combined: *Training takes time.* Time spent by trainers planning for and them implementing training programs. Time spent by the trainees in training instead of doing what they normally do to contribute to the company's goals. Time spent traveling to and from training opportunities. Time for managers to determine individual and group training needs and then follow up on the training to make sure it is being used. Time for re-training when the training wasn't successful, or when something changes. All of this time is part of the cost of doing business, and with a few exceptions there is little that can be done to eliminate or even decrease training time significantly. One of those exceptions is course development.

It takes time to develop training programs as well, usually much more time that it does to deliver them. How much time depends a great deal on how effective you want your program to be. If what you require is training for the simple purpose of saying that the workers have been trained, then effectiveness is not much of an issue. You can institute training that is basically an experienced employee, in training jargon we call them subject-matter experts or SMEs, talking at the trainees about how to do their jobs. When this occurs one-on-one at the job site, it is often termed on-the-job training (OJT). When it happens with the subject-matter expert standing up before a group of trainees in a classroom, it is usually termed a training class. Either way, development time is minimal, although the training it is usually less than adequate and these training delivery techniques belong to the "well, at least we got it done" philosophy of training.

With most training processes, you get out of it what you put into it, which in the above examples isn't much. And please don't think I'm only talking about delivering skills building training for new employees here. How many leadership development programs have been developed and implemented that are basically just a series of internal or external "experts" talking at new leaders and telling them what they should do based solely on what they "think" works, or the current philosophy de jour?

To develop an effective training intervention, one that can lead to real learning and skills mastery by the participants, takes time. That doesn't mean you can't shorten the process considerably though. That's the purpose of this book, to explain how to do training program development right, and as efficiently as possible, using proven techniques and shortcuts that really work.

To achieve this we'll revisit and expand on some of the concepts introduced in this book's companion volume, *Rapid Instructional Design*, and explore a number of new ideas that together will cover the development aspect of various training delivery processes in detail. As you can't talk development without talking training design, some of what we discuss will sound a bit familiar to those of you who have read *Rapid Instructional Design*, but hang in there and we'll get to some stuff that will be new, and hopefully exciting.

WHAT THIS BOOK IS ABOUT

This book is about one phase of the instructional systems design (ISD) model, the one usually labeled "development." If you have some knowledge of ISD, you probably know that the development phase is where you create the course materials that will be used in the next phase, which is usually termed "implementation" or sometimes "delivery." Just in case you aren't familiar with instructional systems design though, or simply to remind you, Figure I.1 shows one of the accepted ISD models.

This model shows the five phases of instructional systems design: Analysis, Design, Development, Implementation, and Evaluation, sometimes referred to as ADDIE, and indicates that the phase we will be discussing, development, comes after design and before implementation.

If you've read *Rapid Instructional Design* though, you might remember that ISD really looks a little more like the model shown in Figure I.2.

Each phase in what I term the Spider Web Model of ISD is interconnected with all other phases as you create your training, so that at any time you might jump back to a previously completed phase or jump ahead to do some thinking about a phase yet to come. This reality, rather than the sequential theory of the first diagram, is going to cause us a few problems as we discuss the development phase, but we'll work our way through them as best we can.

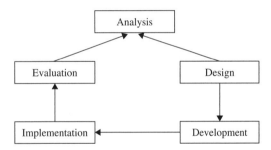

Figure I.1. Instructional Design Cyclic Model

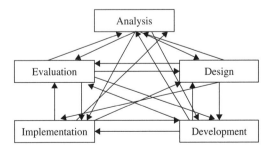

Figure I.2. Instructional Design Spider Web Model

IMPLEMENTATION VS. DELIVERY

The first of these problems is that we will mostly be discussing delivery systems as we explore the rapid techniques of the development phase. Delivery systems are the various ways we get training to our learners. They include approaches such as classrooms, web-based learning, on-the-job training, self-directed learning, mobile learning, and even more esoteric processes such as knowledge management and electronic performance support systems.

If you didn't know a lot about instructional design, you might guess that such concepts would be explored and finalized during the implementation phase of ISD, when according to definition we "deliver" the training. If so, you'd have guessed wrong. (That's what you get for guessing.) How we develop materials, and the shortcuts we can utilize, are to a great extent dependent upon the delivery system that we will implement in the implementation phase, so the delivery decision must be made before you develop your training materials.

If you know a little more about instructional design, you might determine that we need to make the delivery decision sometime during the design phase, and in this case you'd be right (not a guess but some good deductive reasoning). When we begin the development phase, we must already have decided which delivery system we will be using.

We won't be discussing how we make a delivery decision in this book, as it is outside our scope. If you need more information on this topic, *Rapid Instructional Design* or any other good design book can supply it to you.

Another problem is that, while we know we need a delivery decision before we begin development, we aren't always sure exactly what else we may be starting the development process with. Some instructional systems design proponents suggest that writing the learner objectives is the first step in development. Others think this task belongs in the design phase. Some prefer to see learner evaluation (most often you can read that as "test questions") as part of development; others believe that the creation of learner evaluation measures belongs in design. And don't forget the spider web. No matter where you create anything in ISD, there is always a chance you will need to revise some or all of it as you work toward the completion of your program.

For the purpose of this book we will assume that, as you enter the development phase, you, or someone, has created both good learner-centered objectives and properly designed learner-evaluation items for the program. These learner-evaluation items might be criterion-based test questions or some type of performance checklists.

However, as we will soon see, one general and very useful rapid development technique is to begin by creating the learner evaluation, and then building in reverse, so you develop materials, and even the learner objectives based on the evaluation itself.

START AND STOP POINTS

So where does that leave us? Actually, it really doesn't matter. If you subscribe to the spider web model of ISD, the boundaries between all of the phases are pretty fluid, and trying to set them specifically is like trying to decide who owns what part of a maundering and constantly changing river like the Mississippi, simply an exercise in futility.

So we will arbitrarily state for the purposes of this book that generally course development begins when you have a validated set of learner objectives and the learner evaluation items that reflect them. It ends when changes are made to the program and program materials based on the course pilot, and you are ready, we hope, to implement the program.

HOW THIS BOOK IS ORGANIZED

The organization of this book is somewhat different from its companion volume, *Rapid Instructional Design*. In that book we discussed the entire instructional design process and used icon-noted sidebars to provide hints for making each aspect more rapid. Because we covered the process of course development there in detail, we won't spend too much time on the basics here. Instead, the main focus of this volume is on the rapid development techniques themselves, and on how to use them effectively. There will be some review of development basics at the beginning of each chapter, but only enough to get you started and make the rapid development techniques clearer where required.

In *Rapid Instructional Design* we also included icon-noted sidebars for hints that were more useful for occasional designers and techniques that should only be attempted by seasoned practitioners. In this volume there is no differentiation, as all of the rapid development shortcuts are quite usable by anyone, no matter how much development experience he or she has.

Chapter 1 considers various general rapid development techniques, that is, development shortcuts that can be used in almost any delivery system. Some of these are reconsidered in the following chapters when they are of particular value or efficiency in a specific delivery system.

Each of the rest of the chapters focuses on one particular delivery system, first reviewing the development entry and exit points for that system, and then discussing possible rapid development techniques as they relate to the end products of each delivery system's development process.

For example, Chapter 2 on face-to-face classroom deliveries is divided into rapid development hints for the development of Instructor Guides, Participant Packages, and Media, the three major end-products of classroom material development.

You will find that some of the rapid development techniques will appear in more than one delivery system, but we will try to clarify these situations for you when they occur.

Also, a few of the delivery systems themselves function as rapid development techniques, either alone or in conjunction with other deliveries. When this occurs we'll discuss these possibilities first, then consider the delivery systems' own internal rapid development shortcuts based on their end-products.

The final chapter discards this model in favor of brief discussions on concepts that are not major delivery processes, but still play significant roles in training and so require development. These include concepts such as knowledge management and mobile learning.

A colleague of mine once noted that development is the thing that anyone who teaches has to do before he can teach. Even if you can't spell analysis, don't know a learner-based objective (LBO) from an unidentified flying object (UFO), and think tests, like Trix, are for kids, if you instruct you invariably need to develop some type of learning materials, even if they are only lesson outlines in your head. I hope this book can help you to see the importance of getting those things out of your head and into a format in which your learners can use them as quickly and effectively as possible.

Chapter 1

General Rapid Development Techniques

As we've already said, most rapid development techniques depend on the type of delivery system you have determined will work best for your training. However, some are effective in a number of deliveries, or are just so darn basic to the development process that they are the good old "no brainers."

NEED TO KNOW IS WHAT'S NEEDED

One of the most basic of these, although at times even the best course developers get off track and forget it, is the concept of "need to know" versus "nice to know." There is usually a great deal of content that might be covered as you develop your material, and usually not enough time to cover it all, particularly if you plan on adding some of those pesky but so important learner exercises and activities. Even if you did a good job of creating tight objectives back during the design phase, you still need to differentiate between what a learner must really know to be successful in meeting those objectives and what is interesting, but not critical.

Keeping your material development focused on only this "need to know" information means that you don't waste time developing material that you will delete later during the pilot stage when you find you have no time to teach it and realize that it really wasn't all that terribly important anyway. You couldn't ask for a better rapid development technique than simply not developing materials because there is no need to, and this works no matter what delivery process you are using. Stick to developing what the learner really needs to learn (and not what you think is "neat"). You'll never go far wrong, and you'll go right more rapidly.

DON'T REINVENT THE WHEEL

You've heard this old adage before, but it is a really effective rapid development technique. Before you develop your own materials, search around for best practices, for stuff that has already been developed and that you can appropriate (legally. of course). In these days of the web, communities of practice, and even blogs, there is a lot of good material already developed, just sitting out there waiting for you to make it your own. Some may require a little alteration, but that takes a lot less time than developing it yourself from scratch.

As an example, for a program I recently developed for a client on cultural sensitivity, which I knew very little about, my research led me to a website created by a wonderful expert on the topic. He had objectives, an expanded outline, and even a few activities that had been proven successful. I had my clients annotate the outline I retrieved from this website, indicating those areas they thought most important, revised the objectives to reflect their thoughts, and then used the revised objectives, outline, and activities to develop course materials specifically related to the clients' needs, in about one-quarter of the time I would have spent doing it in the usual way, with task analysis and subject-matter experts, followed by laborious material development.

There is plenty of good stuff (and unfortunately plenty of bad stuff as well) available out there that can help shorten your development time, if you only take a little time to search for it. Do a Google search, do an old-fashioned literature search, ask a blog or a community of practice. Forget the "not invented here" syndrome and use this material as a whole, or just pieces; but to take advantage of it, you have to look for it.

WORKING BACKWARD

Another general rapid course development technique that can work in almost any situation is to start at the end, at least the end of the development phase, and work backward. In this case, the question you should ask yourself is, "What do I need to deliver when I implement my course?" There are a number of ways to answer this question, although the fullness of the answer will most often be based on the amount of design work, or at least design thinking, you have done. The answer might range from a brief (very brief) statement of the content, to a formal series of goals for the training, to simply a declaration of the title and the delivery system, for example; "A Web-Based Program on Leadership."

This answer, short as it is, provides you with the two most important things you need to know in the development process, what the course generally entails and how you will deliver it. Arguably it doesn't tell you a lot about either of these key factors, but it is enough to get your development started.

The type of content (leadership, management skill building, technical skills development, familiarization, such as in an orientation program, computer skills, etc.) tells you about what your training content will be like, the objectives you created during design phase providing the details. Meanwhile, knowing the delivery system puts you on a particular development pathway, automatically giving you data such as the need for trained facilitators, depth of material development, type of visuals required, evaluation formats that you can utilize, and much more. With the answers to these questions in hand and the products of a well-done design phase, you have enough to begin course development or to find already developed materials that will work for you.

WORKING BACKWARD: PART TWO

A second rapid development technique that also involves working backward is one we've already mentioned, starting with the learner evaluation and developing the materials based on it. This is a lot more complicated than the previous shortcut—and more complex than it might seem at first glance. First, you need to have a learner evaluation completed, and it must be done properly, that is, criterion based and validated. If your design process ended with the production of the objectives, you will need to create the learner evaluation before you can proceed. You can still use this approach as a rapid development technique; it's just not quite as rapid.

The main advantage of developing materials based on the learner evaluation is that you create only "need to know" materials, and in the form required by the evaluation. Obviously (we hope), if it's on the test it's important, so that means it's "need to know."

The form aspect is a bit less clear to see, unless you have developed a significant number of learner evaluations and understand the difference between cognitive and performance evaluations. Using the normal "work forward" approach, developers often add a lot of cognitive material to a learning process that is mostly performance based. This material, while it seems important, is usually "nice to know" and less critical to the completion of, and so-called learning of, a performance.

For example, it might be nice to know how a mercury thermometer works, but if the task to be evaluated is to determine the temperature of a non-miscible solution, knowing how to mix the solution, take the temperature at the boundary layer, and read the thermometer are much more critical.

A good performance evaluation for this task would require the learner to take the temperature properly and probably ask nothing about how a thermometer works. Developing backward would allow you to recognize this immediately, while developing forward might mean that you never catch this inclusion of unnecessary material at all, or at best not recognize it until you've spent the time creating nice time-consuming diagrams and PowerPoints of how a thermometer functions.

DEVELOPMENT TEAMS

Developing materials through a team approach can be an effective rapid development technique, if you have a team. A development team is almost a requirement in asynchronous web-based learning deliveries, which we will discuss later, but it can be used with some success in other deliveries as well.

One common team approach is to have someone who is good at graphics, or a real PowerPoint enthusiast, do the visuals, while others develop the print content, evaluations, etc. Another less common team approach is to break the program into modules and give each team member one or more modules to develop separately. It doesn't even matter whether the team is in the same location, as computers and web meetings allow them to work and meet from just about anywhere.

If you use this rapid development technique, be sure you have a strong style guide so that everything looks the same when you pull it together and a development checklist to ensure that every team member develops all the pieces that need to be developed. Having templates helps in team development as well, as does planning development milestones so that everyone stays roughly within the same time frame. It's not much of a rapid development technique if 80 percent of your program has been developed but one of the teams fell behind and will take three additional weeks to finish.

Speaking of style guides, having a good one is another rapid development technique all on its own, not only in team development, but anytime you don't want to waste hours thinking about the basics of how a slide should look or what format you want your participant package to come out in.

I've seen all sorts of style guides, small ones, huge ones, ones based on this model or that, and my best recommendation for using one as a rapid development technique is to keep it as simple as possible. Add to your minimal style guide a series of templates for the various end-products of whatever delivery systems you use, and you have a eminently useful document, as well as a great rapid development shortcut.

VENDORS AS RAPID DEVELOPMENT SHORTCUTS

This is another no brainer, though it is one that comes in a few different flavors, depending on your development needs. Basically, if you can afford to have someone else develop your material, you don't need to spend the time doing it yourself. "Duh!"

Those flavors I mentioned though make this rapid development technique a bit more interesting than simply outsourcing. The "plain vanilla" flavor of using a vendor as a rapid development technique is to find someone who has already produced content that matches your objectives and buy it. Even if the content is only close, buy it anyway, and modify it to meet your needs. Be sure to ask the vendor for permission before you do.

A more exotic flavor is to use a vendor's knowledge of the content, how to develop materials, or both if you find the perfect one, to literally develop custom materials for you. The right vendor should be able to develop your materials faster, better, and cheaper than you can. I know the common wisdom is that you can't have all three, but if you find the right vendors they should be faster than you alone as they will usually have a team available to work on your project; better, as they may have experience with the content that you don't, and certainly more experience in development; and even cheaper, as we sometimes forget to factor in all the ancillary costs that come with material development, such as subject-matter expert time, review and pilot time, copy costs, binding costs. . . .

The right vendor can start work immediately, won't be pulled off the job to work on something else because the CEO came up with a "special" idea, and can add more resources more quickly if needed than you probably can, since the vendor doesn't need to go through all your hiring procedures. The key to making all this work, of course, is constant communication between you and the vendor, in both directions.

Now you might be thinking that using vendors/consultants to create a custom training program isn't such a novel idea, but remember that we are talking materials development here, not an entire instructional design. In this model you are still responsible for the

analysis and design work, as well as the implementation and evaluation of your program. You're only requisitioning help in developing
the learning materials, whatever they may be, which is what development is all about. Because you will use your own expertise and
corporate knowledge where it is most effective, during analysis
and design, the process will be a heck of a lot cheaper and more
efficient than hiring a consultant to create an entire program for you
from start to finish.

A slightly different flavor of vendor-based development shortcut
is to hire only the vendor personnel you need for specific purposes,
for example, to develop a specialized simulation that they have the
experience in but you do not, or simply to do your graphics, or even
final editing. There are many specialized resources available to you
as you develop your course, and hiring any one of them can be a
time-saving rapid development technique.

A more specialized flavor is to use vendor instructors to facilitate
your program, particularly if they helped create it or the materials that
are in it. This might not be a true rapid development technique, as
instructing is part of the implementation phase of ISD, but the training of instructors to facilitate a particular course comes under development, as we will see in the next chapter. If you can hire trained
instructors from a vendor, ones who already know the content and
are well-experienced facilitators, you've saved development time that
would have been spent training your own instructors, and so you have
another rapid development technique.

An even more specialized example of this type of rapid development technique is exemplified by a situation I found myself in once
as a training director. My instructional designers and I had developed
a leadership program with the help of a vendor we had worked with
often. When we were getting close to piloting, the vendor's project
manager came to me and opined that my plan of having my designers, who were also good facilitators, facilitate the program might be
questionable. He said he didn't believe they had the background and
content experience to teach this course.

After some further thought and a rousing "We agree" from my
designers, I realized he was right. My people had never been managers and would have had a difficult time relating to some of the
management processes we had developed for the course. I took
the consultant's recommendation and hired two of his top-flight
management trainers to be our facilitators. It would have taken me
many hours of coaching to ready my staff for the facilitation, while

his facilitators came right in and went to it. Of course, I had my folks sit in on a few of the classes, and over time they became confident enough to teach it themselves, but that's not really a rapid development technique, and is certainly another story.

Here are some characteristics of top-shelf vendors/consultants that might help you make up your mind if you're thinking of using one as a rapid development shortcut.

Top Vendor/Consultant Characteristics

- Has a good track record with references
- Gathers plenty of information on your needs and your company before recommending a delivery process or even a piece of one
- Is proficient in a number of authoring products
- Uses the most up-to-date software
- Uses sound instructional design
- Defines things the way you do
- Has the same high standards that you do
- Uses technology that is readily available
- Has a strong development team
- Provides good customer communications
- Knows the steps that lead to the completion of your project
- Provides a quote that is not too high or low compared to others
- Does custom learning development as main function, not a sideline
- Is flexible
- Is located where it is best for you, not for them
- Will spend as much time as you require on-site.
- Has web conferencing facilities if needed
- States that rights to the program are solely yours
- Can provide maintenance and revision services if needed
- Can handle translations if required
- Doesn't tell you that he or she can turn your trainers into developers in practically no time
- Has trained instructional designers on staff
- Exhibits the creativity of the staff

- Has experienced storyboard developers if required
- Has experienced graphics designers if required
- Has an in-house programmer with excellent skills
- Can do ROI and CBA for you if requested
- Is "comfortable" for you

GAMES, A SPECIAL RAPID DEVELOPMENT TECHNIQUE WITH A SPECIAL RESOURCE

One rapid development technique that is useful anywhere, but is for the most part associated with classrooms, is games. Games can be used as activities after the content has been presented or they can themselves present significantly large blocks of content when done with a strong debriefing. If you need to develop specialized games, you tend to lose some of their gain in development time, but if you can use games that have already been developed, and into which you basically insert your content, the development time savings can be substantial. Some of these games even have built-in scorekeeping and timing mechanisms. My friend and esteemed colleague Thiagi terms these types of games *Framegames* and has any number of them for you to borrow and make your own on his website, Thiagi.com.

While best known as classroom materials, games can also be used as a rapid development technique in asynchronous web-based learning, and there are a few now appearing in synchronous web-based deliveries as well. These delivery systems and their attendant rapid development techniques will be discussed in more detail in later chapters.

If you need to develop your own games Learningware and Games2Train are two popular vendors of game development tools.

REPURPOSING

One of the more common rapid development techniques is repurposing, that is, taking a course that was created for one type of delivery and redeveloping the material for a different delivery. Repurposing became the concept of the moment early on in computer based training, and again when synchronous web-based training first appeared on the scene. Many vendors touted their ability to take your classroom programs and turn them into computer based, or later web-based programs. Some did this very well, others not so well. We will be discussing repurposing of various development pieces and parts all through this book, so we'll not detail it now, but here is a fairly extensive list of items to consider if you are thinking of using repurposing as a rapid development technique for creating asynchronous web based training from your classroom materials.

Questions to Ask When Considering Repurposing

- Will the end-users be comfortable with the new delivery format?
- Will their supervisors support the end-users during implementation?
- Will the current instructors support the course?
- Does the current course require a change of delivery?
- Is standardization or consistency important?
- Are there high-level management sponsors for the conversion?
- Is the current delivery taking the learners away from the job for too long?
- Do the learners say the course is too long?
- Do you need to train large numbers in a short time?
- Is the continuing target audience large?
- Is there convenient hardware access?
- Are qualified instructors hard to find or keep?
- Will this repurposing reduce transportation and housing costs for learners?
- Is the content strongly cognitive?
- Is interpersonal interaction required to learn the content?
- Is hands-on equipment required?
- Can simulations be used effectively?
- Is frequent practice required?
- Is behavior modeling required?
- Are the course objectives not being met with the present delivery?
- Does the required software reside where it is needed?
- Is there a budget for things that do not currently exist?
- Do learners in the course vary widely in ability?
- Does the course target entry-level employees?
- Are the learners self-directed?
- Is documentation and record-keeping a problem?

- Is recertification required?
- Is tracking of learner progress important?
- Is there need for course security?

OTHER GENERAL RAPID DEVELOPMENT TECHNIQUES

There are any number of other general rapid development techniques, some of which are more efficient for one delivery or another, but all of which can be effective in various delivery environments. Here's a quick hints list for how to use some of the most effective ones:

- *Use prerequisites to decrease the amount of content you have to create.* This is actually more a design process, but by deciding that the learners will be required to come to the training with some basic knowledge (and letting them know that in advance, don't forget), you will be able to reduce the amount of content development.

- *Use your expanded outline as an instructor guide, combined with the very minimum of learner materials, and keep revising.* This hint is from the "you'll never get it perfect anyway" school of thought. Start with the least development that you can and continuously upgrade the materials every time you do a delivery, based on what you learned during that delivery. You can even add ideas generated by the learners during the class to your materials.

- *Utilize materials that were not created specifically for instruction.* This might include books, chapters from books, magazine articles, websites, manuals, videos, corporate websites, even television programs. I once used excerpts from the various "Star Trek" shows to discuss leadership skills and saw a wonderful example of a person using positive approaches to giving negative feedback on a show called "Project Runway" that I can't wait to try out in a management class. We'll discuss some specific uses of non-instructional materials as rapid development techniques in later chapters, but such pieces can save you development time in almost any learning environment. One caveat to this technique though: Be very aware of the copy-right laws.

- *Use computers.* This may seem like a blinding flash of the obvious in this day and age when computers are so pervasive, but we often miss some of their possibilities. Check out the specialized development software available to see whether it can reduce your development time, think about how general software such as that used for flowcharting or creating spreadsheets might be effective, or create your own computer-based templates for your material development. Even office software like PowerPoint and Word can reduce development time when used effectively.

- *Use subject-matter expert focus groups for reviews.* Instead of sending your materials around to various subject-matter experts for review, hold a focus group review where all the subject-matter experts meet together This not only gives you better control of the time they take to do reviews, but also allows them to all agree on a final version of the materials without the materials going back and forth among the SMEs a number of time-consuming times.

- *Borrow from the best.* When you see a program that you like and that you think worked really well, do a quick outline of how it worked (not the content but the instruction), then develop a file of these outlined ideas that you can reference when developing your own material. You can do this for learner materials you come across that you feel are "top shelf" as well, outlining how the materials were made or simply noting what it was that you liked about them and how you might use them.

RAPID PROTOTYPING

There is one more rapid development technique that we should mention, a concept known as rapid prototyping. Rapid prototyping is one of those slippery concepts that sounds like a good idea when someone talks about it generally, but when it comes down to actually explaining how to do it, you find it hard to express, as it has a number of permutations. That's not to say it isn't a good idea; it is, but it's just sort of hard to describe.

The theory behind rapid prototyping is to recognize that your end-product is simply too complicated to try to make it perfect the first time, before anyone sees it, or the second time, or even the third. Instead, do a quick example of what you are planning to accomplish and see how the decision-makers and others react to it. Then make corrections and go on from there. Now this goes against the grain of almost every instructional designer ever born. We all want our programs to be perfect before anyone sees them. However, in rapid prototyping the 80/20 rule is in effect, and close is more than good enough.

This approach was first used in a training environment by developers working on computer-based learning projects where finding out that the client wasn't pleased after you'd completed all of the programming and graphics was an invitation to disaster, not to mention a waste of large amounts of development time. Instead, they would create small pieces of the final project that exhibited aspects such as screen design, learner interface, activities, content, etc. Then, as the client saw and approved these, they could go on and complete the program, incorporating those characteristics that passed the test.

A slightly different concept of rapid prototyping is to take a small piece of the whole program content and finish it completely, including the interfaces, visuals, testing, basically creating a small working model. After approval of this model the other pieces are created and assembled.

Still a third notion uses the above approach, but for each program piece. As a piece is completed, it is considered and either selected or rejected. Selected pieces are assembled into a larger piece, and that piece goes through the same selection process until the final program is complete. Rejected pieces are kept in a file for possible use in another program.

Some rapid prototypes are created simply to obtain agreement on color schemes, fonts, and screen characteristics, others to exhibit interfaces and navigation. When expressly created for theme or color decisions, they are often done using static graphics software instead of the delivery software, which is more difficult to program, thus saving even more development time.

There are possibilities for rapid prototyping as a rapid development technique in most of the major delivery systems, although it obviously is most effective in asynchronous web-based programs. As with all our general rapid development techniques, keep it in mind when you are planning any major program development, and use it whenever it will work for you.

Chapter 2

Rapid Classroom Course Development

Entry and Exit for Development
- Begin with validated objectives, a topic outline, and an expanded outline. Learner evaluation questions may be completed, or they may be created during the development process.
- End with pilot of classroom and a train-the-trainer session.

End Products
- Instructor Guide
- Participant Package
- Media
- Learner Evaluations

As far as specific rapid development techniques go, we'll talk about classrooms first. Why? Because even after all the technology of the past half-century, and all the soothsayers who predicted the classroom's demise, stand-up training, or instructor-led training (ILT), or face-to-face training (F2F), or whatever you want to call it, is still the most common delivery method used by trainers. That's not to say it is the most common form of training. That honor goes to unstructured on-the-job training, where a subject-matter expert basically tells a new colleague what he or she needs to know to do the job. We won't be discussing unstructured on-the-job training here, as it is at best a questionable delivery system, and at worst an unacceptable substitute for real training.

That being said, back to the delivery system most trainers use most often (and most people picture most often when you mention training), live, face-to-face classrooms. As noted above, classroom training has any number of titles and about as many definitions and conceptualizations. To keep it simple, we'll define classroom training here as training that occurs away from the job (it doesn't need to be too far away) in which a group of learners physically meet and work with an instructor in a room designated for that purpose. That word "instructor" is the key to rapid classroom course development.

To be effective, all classroom interventions, whether for training, education, or whatever, require an instructor, who in turn requires an instructor guide. Most often the classroom program also requires a participant package, and in some cases quite a lot more in the way of materials, but it is the instructor guide that involves the most development time and has the most possibilities for rapid development shortcuts.

The participant package can be as simple as a list of the course objectives or as complex as a technical manual and has its own rapid development shortcuts. We'll discuss this aspect a bit later, and focus on the instructor guide first.

INSTRUCTOR GUIDE RAPID DEVELOPMENT TECHNIQUES

The instructor guide (lesson plan, instructor notes, facilitator package, etc.) can be as simple as some notes, or as complicated as the directions for putting together your child's bicycle, depending on a number of variables, but to use any of its rapid course development methods effectively, the important first step is to consider your instructor, or instructors as the case may be.

One-Man Band

If you are not only the course developer but also the only instructor for the training, you may be able to use the rapid development technique of reducing your instructor guide to nothing more formal than a bare-bones topic outline or expanded outline, with perhaps a few extra notes concerning activities you plan to do or other non-content-related ideas. Understanding this can save you hours of work spent creating a full-blown instructor guide that is not required for the training, as no one will ever use it but you. Such an instructor guide might look something like the one in Figure 2.1.

FACILITATION SKILLS COURSE

Content	Media, Activities, Notes
I. Icebreaker A. *Ferris Bueller* This is interaction but not facilitation	*Ferris Bueller* excerpt
B. Worst experience as a learner	Flip Chart 2. Three defining characteristics all had in common Do as small groups Each group votes for best of worst in group to report to main group
C. Best Instructor	Flip chart Do as large group One characteristic from each Note that these characteristics are those of a Facilitative Instructor
II. Introductions and Objectives A. Overview 1. The art and science of instruction	PPT Slide 2
B. Introductions	Use two truths and a lie

Figure 2.1. Reduced Instructor Guide

As you might expect, there are a couple of caveats to this particular rapid development technique. The first is that you need to be an SME to make such a reduced instructor guide work. This is usually the case if you are the instructor as well as the developer, but I have seen and been part of program development where the developer is the instructor but not really an SME. In this case you will at least want to add into your instructor guide some of the ideas the subject-matter experts gave you while you were working through the content with them, and maybe a little more description of the concepts you are not too familiar with.

A second reason you might not want to develop a minimal instructor guide is that your boss, or the organization, has a requirement for something more. I did a few years of military training a while ago, and our course developers were often both the course instructors and well-versed subject-matter experts. However, the organization's instructional plan required that every instructor guide follow the exact same model and be very complete, almost a script. The logic of this had to do with the third reason for not developing condensed instructor guides, the concern over what happens if the developer/instructor is ill, otherwise not available, or leaves the organization.

To use an old circus adage, "The Show Must Go On." This is as true for training as it is for an artistic performance, which to some extent is what a stand-up class is. A minimal instructor guide seldom allows another instructor to perform effectively, even if he or she is a subject-matter expert. There is just too little to work with, as most of the really "good stuff" is in the developer/instructor's head. So if it's critical that your training program be delivered when scheduled, whether you're there or not, you may want to think twice about this development shortcut.

Developing Instructor Guides for Other Instructors

If you are the course developer, but not the instructor, you can still utilize the rapid development technique of reducing the size and complexity of your instructor guide, particularly if the instructor will be an SME. Your subject-matter expert won't need much more than your expanded topic outline to remind him or her about the content. You'll probably want to make the directions for your activities a little more complete than you would have for yourself and to spend some time discussing other aspects such as the audience and the objectives, but minimizing content discussion in the instructor guide will save you plenty of development time.

If you know the instructor is also a competent facilitator, you can reduce these delivery aspects as well, almost to the point of creating a series of instructor reminder notes for both the content and the activities that you want to make sure the instructor handles properly. I call this whole approach of fitting the instructor guide to the instructors "Trainer-Based Development," as you create the instructor guide based on what the trainer who will be doing the instruction needs. It will serve you well as a rapid development technique under the proper circumstances.

The real problems begin when you have multiple instructors, particularly if one of those instructors is you. One of the most common mistakes developer/instructors make is to create an instructor guide that works for them, but is less than effective for other instructors who teach the material. I've lost count of the number of times I've picked up an instructor guide developed by a very competent developer/instructor and found myself unable to use it, even though

I had the subject-matter expertise. As in any course development, the issue here is to remember your audience, although in this case the audience is not the participants, but the other instructors.

This doesn't mean you need to create a fully detailed instructor guide each time a number of other instructors are going to use your course material. It does mean that you are going to need to do a little "instructor analysis" to find out what your colleagues will need, and more importantly for rapid course development, what they won't require.

To accomplish this you'll need to at least talk to them. Better yet, have them help you in the development by reviewing a prototype instructor guide and asking for their feedback. Be careful though to focus their feedback on the format and depth of the guide. If they are SMEs, or think they are, you'll mostly get comments on the content otherwise, which is OK for content reviews, but not here.

You'll also want to determine their level of subject-matter expertise to help guide you in the content depth of the instructor guide. As noted earlier, there is lots of time to be saved if you don't need to explain every aspect of every piece of content.

Developing Detailed Instructor Guides

Another type of instructor audience you may encounter is one in which you have multiple instructors who are not SMEs, or you just don't know enough about them to be sure. This is often the case if you are a consultant developing course materials for a client's instructors to teach or if you are creating materials that might be used by any number of people across a large corporation. An example of this that I always find a challenge is developing material for a new human resources initiative that will be taught not only by trainers, but also by HR representatives, some of whom have subject-matter skills but no instructional skills, and others who have neither to any great extent.

The instructor guide you need to develop in this case must be as detailed as possible, in some cases almost a script, providing everything the instructors will say and the participants will be asked to do. Here is an example of what I mean.

These instructor guides leave little room for error, or unfortunately, creativity, and there are not many ways to do them rapidly. On the positive side, almost anyone with even a smattering of content knowledge can use them effectively . . . if they follow them, which is another whole story.

Fully detailed instructor guides like the one in Figure 2.2 are often used by large companies to ensure that their training is consistent, no

PERFORMANCE OBJECTIVES

Block Time	Activity	Step	Key Points/Transitions	Flip Charts/Overheads/Handouts
:25	Review/Preview	1	Purpose: • To review the content from Day 1 • To overview the agenda for Day 2 Transition: "Today is about providing direction through performance objectives and essential management practices directly linked to our leadership competencies."	Agenda OH 1
:25	Presentation and Discussion: Providing Direction: Setting Objectives	2	Purpose: • To build value for the importance of setting and communicating performance objectives in today's business context • To overview and have participants practice using SMART Transition: "To have a solid understanding of the criteria for ensuring useful objectives that contribute to business results, let's put this knowledge to the test and create some examples of SMART objectives from your own environment."	Providing Direction OH 2 Providing Direction OH 3 Why Don't Employees Always Do What They Are Supposed to Do? OH 4 Why Don't Employees Always Do What They Are Supposed to Do? OH 5 SMART Objectives OH 6 Specific OH 7 Measurable OH 8 Achievable OH 9 Relevant OH 10 Time-Bound or Timely OH 11
:25	Partner Group Exercise: SMART Skill Practice	3	Purpose: To practice developing SMART performance objectives Transition: "You'll now have an opportunity to apply this framework to the performance objectives you collected in your Preparation Materials assignment and to receive some feedback from others in the group."	Partner Exercise: Creating SMART Objectives OH 12

Time	Activity	No.	Content	Materials
:35	Trio-Group Exercise: Making Your Employees' Performance Objectives SMARTer	4	Purpose: To apply the SMART criteria to improve some of your employees' individual performance objectives Transition: "Let's take a fifteen-minute break, after which we'll turn our attention to communicating and building commitment to performance objectives."	Trio-Group Exercise: Making Your Employees' Performance Objectives SMARTer OH 13
:15	Break	5		
:15	Lecturette/ Discussion: Communicating Performance Objectives	6	Purpose: To overview a process of communicating, discussing, and building commitment to performance objectives Transition: "Now you will have an opportunity to apply these skills in a simulated environment."	Communicating Performance Objectives OH 14
:90	Putting It All Together—Simulation	7	Purpose: To practice setting and communicating SMART goals and assessing the effectiveness of those goals, based on results Transition: "Let's take the last few minutes to make some plans for taking what you have learned today back to work."	Putting It All Together: Simulation Overview OH 15 Strategy OH 16 Phase 1: Setting and Communicating Performance Goals OH 17 Phase 2: Working to Achieve Results. OH 18 Phase 3: Assessing Results and Providing Feedback OH 19
:20	Summary and Transition Planning	8	Purpose: To develop a plan for setting and communicating performance goals with an employee Transition: "After lunch we will be looking at another core skill for new managers: coaching."	Transition Planning OH 20
:60	Lunch	9		

Figure 2.2. Extended Instructor Guide

matter where in the world it is done or by whom. There is a fallacy here in assuming that all instructors will follow the guide, although this can be overcome through monitoring and strong evaluation.

I once had a problem in a company I worked for as a curriculum manager when my instructors would only use the instructor guides when someone was "watching," so to speak. If they were not being critiqued, they often went "off the reservation" with their war stories and forays into content that was certainly interesting, but didn't help the learners master the objectives. I solved this situation by periodically appearing at the end of a class, taking a few learners aside, and asking them to look at the instructor guide and tell me if the instructor followed it. Often they would say yes, just to protect the instructor, but just as often one or two would say no, or would ask what a certain key concept was, as the instructor had not mentioned it. I used this information not to confront the instructor, but to determine how many more times I would be sitting in on the class. The instructors soon got the message and compliance with the instructor guide rose significantly.

In the final analysis, unless you work for an organization in which it is critical that the training be in strict compliance to a set of standards that are reflected in the training material, this type of detailed instructor guide is seldom worth the effort expended in developing it. It becomes a rapid development technique simply to know that you don't have to do it. How much better to give your instructors just what they need in terms of an instructor guide and allow their creativity and knowledge of their learners to fill in the rest. And it makes your course development faster!

Other Rapid Development Techniques for Instructor Guides

There are a number of other ways to make the development of your instructor guides more rapid. The easiest of these is to simply borrow pieces of instructor guides from other courses you've already developed. After you've been developing for a while you'll have many activities, games, and other classroom processes that you can use in multiple classes and that the instructor guides have already been completed for. A good example of this is a favorite icebreaker or summary activity. Once you've created it for an instructor guide, you can simply cut and paste it into another guide where you plan to use it. Sometimes you need to make slight modifications, but you save a lot of typing time, and maybe some thinking time as well.

Other candidates for this treatment include complex management simulations and specialized games that you developed. You may need to change the names and even the scenario to fit a different type of class, but if it is pertinent to the new class, the majority of the simulation can be lifted straight from one instructor guide and placed in another. By the way, this is true as well for participant packages, as we will discuss later.

Speaking of participant packages, another rapid development technique for instructor guides is to develop the participant package first, which most developers consider a somewhat backwards way to do things. For many highly learner centered classes, however, the participant package is the real guide to how the class should be facilitated. Completing the participant package first allows you to use it as a road map for developing the major portion of your instructor guide.

This post-participant package instructor guide should basically be comprised of guidelines on how to facilitate the learner activities, along with a few other directions concerning introductions, summaries, and the mechanics of the class. This technique does not work well if your class is more instructor centered (that is, lecture based), but if this is the case, you might want to consider a redesign. Classrooms that focus on the instructor are seldom places where learning occurs.

Another rapid development technique for instructor guides is to create a template that you start with each time you do a guide. I've seen such templates that were as simple as a couple of empty columns with some titles, and others as complicated as a system in which the developer basically fills in the blanks. I don't recommend this second approach unless your situation requires that every instructor guide look exactly like every other one and that the programs you are creating all work exactly alike, but I've been in training environments where this was the case, and the more standardization we employed the better.

Most often you can create your own personal instructor guide template that falls somewhere between these extremes, with your preferred font and formatting built in and perhaps a number of placeholders for general classroom pieces such as the icebreaker, your introduction, internal and final summaries, and evaluation. Figures 2.3, 2.4, 2.5, 2.6, and 2.7 are some examples of templates that I like to use, depending on the situation.

If you are a newer course developer, there are also a number of development templates in software formats available from various vendors. These templates not only provide a place to transcribe your instructor guide, but also help you to think through the development process itself. As such, they work well as rapid development techniques for those with little or no formal background in course development, but can tend to be a bit constricting for developers who have experience and are used to doing things their own way.

Another problem with these software based templates is that most have been created to help develop e-learning, and therefore do not necessarily give you an instructor guide as a final product. Also, their starting point is usually well before the development phase, sometimes beginning in analysis and requiring you to go through all the steps in the instructional design process in order to populate your development materials. If you've already completed your analysis and design, this makes the use of such software less than acceptable as a rapid development technique. I've included in the suggested resources area the websites for a few of the vendors of this type of software.

PARTICIPANT PACKAGE RAPID DEVELOPMENT TECHNIQUES

As mentioned earlier, the participant package (ne learner guide, course handout, study guide, etc.) can be as simple as a list of the course objectives, or as complex as a technical manual. Actually, a participant package that is basically a technical manual is usually not the best learning tool in most situations, although many new developers often think it is.

Now before you technical skills trainers go off on me complaining that the tech manuals are the most important part of your training, I didn't say you shouldn't use them, I simply stated that, by themselves, they weren't the best way to produce a participant package, nor are they usually a particularly good learning tool.

Instructor Notes	Media and Directions
As the trainee gains proficiency performing the task in an "ideal" environment, on-the-job noise or normal environmental factors are added.	Introduce noise gradually.
Aid the trainee in integrating new subject matter.	Display OH 12.
Use positive reinforcement, i.e., praise the person, criticize the action.	Display OH 14.

Figure 2.3. Two-Column Instructor Guide Template

Participant Package

Adult Learner Assumptions

Assumpions	Pedagogical	Andragogical
The learner is.......	Dependent	Self-directed
The learner's experience is....	Built on more than used as a resource	Used as a resource for learning by self and others
The learner's readiness to learn is.....	Uniform by age level and curriculum	Developed from life's experience
The learner's orientation to learning is......	Subject-centered	Task or problem centered
The learner is motivated by...	External rewards and punishments	Internal incentives and curiosity

Knoles, M. S. (1990)

Adult Learning Principles

1.

2.

3.

4.

5.

6.

7.

8.

9.

Media

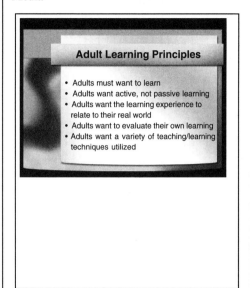

Content

VI. Adult Learning

      A. Pedagogy vs. Andragogy

            1. Assumption Chart

            2. Five Principals

                  a. Not just adult but all learners

Ask: Can you add more principles to the list?

Note the Adult Instructional Design Checklist in the handout as well

Figure 2.4. Three-Part Instructor Guide

Lesson Plan # 221	Program Title: Instructional Design	Revision: 1
# of pages 12	Module Title: Objectives	Time: 4 hours
Time	Media/Activities	Content
45 min.	OH 17 Participant Package, pp. 23–25 Flip Chart	Review page 23 and discuss example 1 Refer to task chart and audience analysis Ask: What do we want them to know 30-minute small group interaction on pulling knowledge from analysis
30 min.	OH 18 Mager, pp.10–21 Participant Package, pp. 26–27	Discuss characteristics of good objectives Complete and discuss activity, page 27
45 min.	LUNCH	LUNCH
60 min.	OH 19–22 Participant Package, pp. 28–32 and addendum 1 Pass out: Verbs	Discuss levels Read Participant Package, pp. 28–30 Discuss parts of objective Conditions Standards Verbs Note: all parts not necessary all the time Complete parts exercise Participant Package, pp. 31–32

Figure 2.5. Three-Column Instructor Guide Template

Technical Manuals As a Rapid Development Technique

Technical specifications and manuals were meant to be reference materials, and as such, are invaluable to both the learner and training program developers as they create classroom programs, but they should be used for the purpose they were intended, as a reference, not as a guide to the participants' learning, which is what a good participant package is.

If you have a technical manual that is related to the training you are developing, your participant package should refer to it, sometimes continuously, but this reference document should not be the participant package itself. Understanding this will help make your course development faster and seriously decrease the size of your participant package as well, making your trainees happier.

We will not spend time discussing the actual development of a participant package here, as that is not the purpose of this book and, depending on the type of class you are developing, there are many different items that might be included, such as forms, readings,

Slide or Medium	Instructor Prompts	Content Outline	Learning Points
Review Slide 27	Refer *to overhead for the term "systemic."* Review *learning points in the right-hand column in your own words, transitioning back to the subject of being systemic as part of the ways and means for delivering better quality and achievement of improved* alignment. State: *Cultures work in non-linear ways.* A culture is like a living thing. Complex relationships influence quality outcomes. We speak of cultural patterns that involve the unique combinations of relationships within an organization. (Do not use slide with condensed version.)	Slide 27 Systemic: • Non-linear relationships among "living" things • Gain understanding by synthesis • Look at system as a whole composed of pieces • Deterministic but not calculable—unpredictable • World as an ecosystem	Learning Point: Think of the human body's various systems and how they are linked systemically. (The seven systems are respiratory, digestive, nervous, reproductive, endocrine, skeletal-muscular, and circulatory.) Learning Points: Synthesis involves "ecological anticipation." Synthesis involves working collaboratively beyond the boundaries of our own knowledge and experience. Synthesis brings together the varied experience and knowledge on a team to reduce performance gaps and create opportunities for process improvements. We need to anticipate the impact of our problem solving.

Figure 2.6. Four-Column Instructor Guide Template

Objective (The trainee will be able to . . .)	Content (Expanded outline)	Methods and Media(Overheads, questions, activities)	Testing (The objective will be met when . . .)

Figure 2.7. Objective-Based Four-Column Template

fill-in-the-blank notes pages, directions for complicated activities, and high-level graphics, just to mention a few. Let's just say that whatever assists your learners in learning is fair game for your participant package, as long as the instructor uses it in class, or at least refers to it as a supplementary piece that may be of interest.

Too often unschooled developers put material in a participant package that has no reason to be there, but simply seemed interesting to them. Magazine articles, unnecessary flow charts, and long lists of reference readings are just some of the items that tend to "junk up" participant packages. Once again the golden rule of participant packages is that, if the instructor is not going to use it or refer to it in class, then it probably does not belong in the package. The companion volume to this book, *Rapid Instructional Design*, has more information on how to create participant packages, but here is a short list of what you might include.

Possible Inclusions in a Participant Package

- Supply lists
- Pre-work assignments (if the trainees will receive their manual before class)
- Objectives
- Introductions
- Reading materials
- Instruments
- Worksheets for skill practice or role plays
- Feedback forms
- Simulation directions
- Case studies
- Directions for activities
- Gaming materials
- Job aids
- Quizzes
- Reference materials
- Bibliography
- Glossary
- Evaluations

- Supplemental materials for enrichment such as magazine articles, related corporate policies or marketing materials, and technical articles or information
- Frequently asked questions (FAQs)

Major Participant Package Rapid Development Techniques

We've already discussed a primary rapid development technique for a participant package: only put in things that are necessary to the learning. This will also make your instructor guide development more rapid, as you will not need to add references and instructions there for participant package materials that have no real purpose in being there, as they do not help the learners master the objectives.

Since what you do put into your participant package is dependent on two major variables, the participants and the content, another rapid development technique is to understand both of these aspects very well before you begin to develop your participant package. Charts and graphs that don't speak directly to the objectives, simulations that are beyond the ability of the learners, or activities that are beneath them, are all major errors that often occur during development. These common mistakes increase the amount of time spent both doing, and then redoing, your participant package when you find out that they are not what you needed because they are not what the learners need. Using the objectives as your content guide (basically, if it doesn't help the learner master an objective, it probably isn't worth the time to develop) and knowing who your learners are and what they are capable of can also help to keep you from spending time redoing your participant package development after the pilot tells you there is simply too much or the wrong kind of information, a rapid development technique if there ever was one.

We've already talked about using the instructor guide to help create your participant package and doing the participant package first as a rapid development technique, but another technique that can be a real development shortcut is to do both the instructor guide and the participant package simultaneously. Using this method you can be pretty much guaranteed that what you have in one is reflected in the other. This also provides a good cross-check to make sure that you haven't added extraneous material to either, particularly to the participant package.

Unfortunately, to do this well requires a significant amount of development experience. It's easy to get confused when doing both at the same time, necessitating going back again . . . and again . . . and again, which wastes a considerable amount of time. For a new developer particularly, it's better to stick to developing either the instructor guide or the participant package first (usually the instructor guide first) and then creating the other based on a finished product.

There are software templates available for participant package development as well as for instructor guides, but as we mentioned, participant packages can vary widely between courses, so use these templates with caution. You might also develop your own participant package template as a rapid development technique, with placeholders for standard requirements such as objectives, course introduction, needed materials lists, course evaluations, suggested readings, etc. The real savings in this template though is the formatting, with font type and size and header/footer requirements set automatically. Such templates are not only a rapid development technique, but will give all of your development products a much more professional and finished look. Here are some ideas for what your participant package template might contain, followed by a few thoughts on good participant package design.

Participant Package Template Inclusions

- Title page
- Table of contents
- Supplies
- Objectives
- Page setups for other types of exhibits
- Company logo
- Font types, size, and colors
- Graphics dimensions

Participant Package Design Considerations

- Use company-approved color schemes and logos.
- Leave plenty of white space (25 percent of the page is not too much).
- Leave space between blocks of content.
- Leave space between headings and text.
- Use only one or two fonts (Times New Roman, Arial, and Helvetica are most common).

- Use 10-point to 14-point type.
- Justify the left margin.
- Use running headers or footers with page number, unit, course and revision numbers, and course title.
- Use simple sentences.
- Stay away from decorative fonts and all caps.
- Be sure that the reference for each pronoun is easily understood.
- Use illustrations instead of words.
- Use highlighting and bold to draw attention to main points.
- Use boxes, but with restraint.
- Check readability.
- Have a table of contents.
- Use a new right-hand page for each major subtopic.
- Number the pages.
- Leave wide margins.
- Use "I" and "you."
- Use the active voice.
- Explain *why* not to do something; don't just say "don't do it."
- Use short sentences with ten to fifteen words.
- Make paragraphs short, with only three to four sentences.
- Beware of:
  - Stereotypes
  - Too much repetition
  - Technical jargon (without definition)
  - Acronyms (without explanation)
- Edit, edit, edit

PowerPoint As a Rapid Development Technique for Participant Packages

One other participant package development shortcut, that I add with some trepidation, is the inclusion of PowerPoint slides in your participant package. This is a really quick way to fatten up your participant package (if that's what you need) and arguably provides an organizer for the learning. I was taught back in the formative years of my career not to put slides (2X2 projector type or overhead projections at that time) into the participant package, as this wasn't the purpose of visual aids, but that was before PowerPoint. The ease of creating PowerPoint slides and hard copy facsimiles of them for a participant package now means that every instructor, professional and non-professional, uses the technique of placing copies of the Power-Point slides in the participant package, and participants have actually come to expect it. In fact, they often get grumpy if you don't do it.

As I said, it does provide a kind of a learning organizer, and it is also a great place for your learners to take notes that they can keep attached to the visuals. You can even make this process more interactive by making the participant package PowerPoint pages as fill-in-the-blank, with key words left out that require the learners to write in and therefore focus on the slides.

Two warnings concerning this process though. First, it tends to make developers think they can "load up" their visuals with text as the learners will have a copy in front of them to read from if they can't see all the words. Wrong! All the old rules for creating visuals still apply, particularly the most basic one: "If all of your learners can't see the slide from any portion of the classroom, you shouldn't project it." They will lose focus, both on the visual and on what you are saying, as they squint their way through your over-texted slides either on the screen or in their participant package. In case you've forgotten, here are some other "old rules" for visuals.

Rules for Developing Static Visuals

- No more than six lines per slide

- No more than six words per line

- Twenty-four point font size or the equivalent is best (eighteen point is the absolute minimum)

- Use both upper and lower case letters—title case, not all caps

- Use either vertical or horizontal format, not both; horizontal (landscape) is usually best

- Use bullets, stars, dashes, and so on

- Each slide should have a title

- Key words are best

- Keep your phrases short and simple

- One main idea per slide. Use builds to add new concepts

- Check your spelling and grammar, then have someone else check it again

- Use graphics where possible (charts, diagrams, line drawings, cartoons), but keep them simple and guard against clutter
- Tables are difficult to read on projected graphics
- Do not add sound or animations without good reason
- Keep backgrounds consistent and subtle
- Use only quality clip art, and use it sparingly
- Check all graphics, especially gradient effects, on the projection system to see how they will look
- Use the chart style that is appropriate for the data
- Light colors on dark backgrounds attract the eye
- Use color cues to imply relationships
- Establish a color scheme at the beginning and stick with it
- Don't overuse boldface or italic
- Sans serif fonts such as Helvetica are easier to read when projected

My other warning is "Don't give away the store." What I mean by this is that if you have question-and-answer sessions in your program, either verbal or written, you need to be careful that you don't include the answers on an upcoming slide. Learners have a tendency to flip through their participant packages, especially the slides. It tends to make self-quizzes or question/answer activities just a bit too easy once they discover that a slide in their participant package has all the answers to your questions. As you might guess, I learned this one through sad experience when I first started putting my Power-Point slides in my participant packages. It did feel good though (until I realized what was happening) to have all my questions answered immediately by most of the class.

PowerPoint as a "Passout"

Perhaps the most useful rapid development technique connected to the use of PowerPoint is to use the hard copy slides as passouts after discussions, both as a summary activity and a retention tool. A passout is a document that you "pass out" at a specific juncture during the class, rather than providing it as a handout, such as in the case of a participant package that you give to the learners at the beginning of the class. Using PowerPoint passouts also means that you can make changes to these documents almost on the fly, as long as you have a copy machine nearby.

Passouts themselves are also a rapid development technique on their own, as using them in the right situation means you don't need to wait for last-minute material to come in from subject-matter experts before you can complete and print your participant package. And if they send you some new update or change, you don't have to spend time editing and recopying the participant package to include the new material. This can be a huge cost savings as well as a time savings for you.

The problem with passouts, of course, is that they are cumbersome, cumbersome to pass out, to carry around with you, and to keep straight while you are instructing. However, I've seen excellent instructors use nothing but passouts in an incredibly effective manner, their learners ending the day with a participant package comprised totally of materials passed out during the class. I'm not suggesting that this for everyone, as these were well-seasoned, very professional instructors who used this technique, but passouts really can cut down on participant package development time, especially when revisions are a constant problem.

Either way, remember that if you do decide to develop passouts for your program, make sure your learners can integrate them into their participant packages easily (a spiral bound participant package is not the right approach for integrating passouts) and that you give the learners time to place them in their participant packages and scan them before you resume your instruction.

PowerPoint Slides As the Instructor Guide

There is one other rapid development technique related to using PowerPoint that you might utilize, but I consider it to be the nuclear option of material development. If you are required to instruct a class or part of a class for which you are not an SME, and you do not have the time to become one or create a good instructor guide, you can use your PowerPoint slides as your instructor notes, reminding you of what you need to do and say as you project them. PowerPoint even has a note facility for this purpose . . . sort of.

As I said, this technique is only for use when desperate times require desperate actions, although I've seen a number of instructors use it as their normal development approach, usually to their and the learners' great disadvantage. I'll say no more about this technique except that you should consider employing it only at your own risk, as under no circumstances does it take the place of proper material development or preparation.

Other Rapid Development Techniques for Your Participant Package

Just a couple of other thoughts for you on shortcuts when developing participant packages.

Always include a Frequently Asked Questions page in your participant package. You can keep adding to this as you find more and more questions, and just having it available will decrease the amount of material you need to create for your participant package, as well as the necessity of doing continuous revisions each time your Level 1 or 2 evaluation indicates the need for added material. This works even better if your frequently asked questions are online so that, instead of revising a print page, you simply revise a website page.

Create an online list of terms and acronyms with definitions. Like your frequently asked questions, putting this list online means you can add to it or change it without the need to reprint your participant package. If you feel the learners will need these lists in class, you can either print them and use them as a passout or ask the learners to do the printing and go over them as a pre-class activity before bringing them to class.

CLASSROOM ACTIVITIES AS A RAPID DEVELOPMENT TECHNIQUE

Because most well-designed classroom programs are loaded with learner activities, any way in which you can decrease the amount of time spent developing these activities can lead to real efficiencies in both time and costs. We've already mentioned one possibility, repurposing activities that you have already created for another face-to-face class. Especially if the activity is complex and requires a lot of instructions, this can be a great timesaver.

If the activity was previously developed for a face-to-face classroom delivery, you should be able to cut and paste it right into the new program. If it was developed for another type of delivery system (web-based, OJT, etc.) it may take a little rebuilding and reshaping to fit the classroom environment, although it shouldn't take near as much time as building an activity from scratch.

Just as effective a rapid development technique is employing ready-to-use activities that have been developed by others.

This might include activities developed by your colleagues in the organization, by other training professionals, or by vendors.

The obvious advantages here are that you have a much wider selection of possibilities to choose from and you don't need to spend the time developing them in the first place. Disadvantages include your unfamiliarity with how the activities actually work in a class and only employing ones that have been developed properly. There is also a cost factor involved, as most of the best of these activities are not free.

Just like your own activities, some of those developed by others will need to be retooled to meet your needs. You may even find that it's only the concept of the activity that you want to use and decide to revise it completely to speak more directly to your learners.

Specialized Activity-Based Rapid Development Techniques

There are a few specialized ways to use activities as rapid classroom development techniques. For example, instead of developing summaries with PowerPoint slides and participant package information, I like to have the learners create the summaries as an activity, sometimes as presentations or as a series of questions that they present to the class or ask each other in smaller groups. You can use "Ah Ha" lists as well for a summary, where the learners jot down particularly important things they learn as the class progresses and then share them at the end.

Introductory activities in which the learners provide the information in the form of needs, objectives, or simply reasons why they are in class can also reduce development time. Basically, the more you involve the learners in supplying their own knowledge, the less you need to create material, and it's good adult learning theory too!

The Framegames we discussed in the general rapid development technique area are another type of specialized learner activity that can save you classroom development time, as are an entire universe of tests and instruments that are available in various books, Pfeiffer *Annuals*, etc. Basing a block of content on one of these instruments when it is applicable usually means your material development is reduced to debriefing questions and a summary.

Sources of Activities

There are any number of sources for classroom activities that you can use as part of your rapid development process. As mentioned, your colleagues may have some that they developed and are willing to share. You can find others that are free for the taking on various websites. Even some consultant websites have free activities to share. The best of these as far as I'm concerned are Thiagi.com and Don Clark alias Big Dog at www.nwlink.com/~donclark/hrd.html

Entire books full of classroom activities and games are available, as well as the Pfeiffer *Annuals* and other periodicals that provide you with copyright-free and very customizable scenarios, role plays, instruments, and other classroom activities. See the Suggested Resources list at the back of this book for some of the many possibilities.

Of course, many of the best activities are those developed by vendors. There are plenty of these as well, ranging from short icebreakers to complex simulations that take hours to complete. There are two problems with vendor activities. The first is that, naturally, you have to pay for them. If you have the money this isn't a problem. If you don't, it still isn't much of a problem because you just can't use them, so you find or develop something else.

Even if you have the money, be very careful that you know what you are paying for. Many a trainer has bought an activity or even an entire program from an off-the-shelf vendor assuming they could use it at any time in any way, only to find that there was an additional charge for each set of materials or for each learner. This can easily mean that the money you thought you had isn't enough.

The second problem with vendor-supplied activities for use as rapid development shortcuts is that you may or may not be permitted to change them. This goes back to the "Be careful that you understand what you are paying for" concept. Some vendors sell you a license to use their material, but not to change it. Just because you paid them for the activity doesn't mean that you have bought their copyright. Even very small changes can lead to very large problems. Be sure that you clarify with the vendor what you are allowed and not allowed to change, and if their rules are too strict, find someone else who is more flexible.

I've never actually run into this problem myself. Most vendors are happy to allow you to "fiddle" with their activities and will even ask for a copy of what you've changed if they think they can use it for other clients. For example, when I was working in health care I took a series of supervisory activities that I had purchased from a vendor and retooled them for the health care environment. My agreement with the vendor was that they in turn could sell the activities with my changes to other health care organizations.

VENDOR PROGRAMS AS A RAPID DEVELOPMENT TECHNIQUE

Talking about vendors brings up one of the most rapid classroom development techniques of all, simply buying an entire off-the-shelf program from a vendor. This can include all the materials, and even the instructors. All the things we've already mentioned concerning vendor-supplied activities goes double for this rapid development technique. Naturally, you want to make sure what you are buying meets your learners' needs and your objectives, and that the price includes what you think it does as far as materials reproduction and number of learners who can be enrolled.

Vertical market courseware supplies such as MC Strategies for healthcare and Kaplan Financial for finance training can also be tremendous sources of programs that can reduce your development time if your work is in their area of expertise.

Most importantly, you need to be clear as to what you are allowed to do with the program. With a little tweaking here and there, a good vendor program can become a rapid development shortcut for a number of your training needs, and pieces of it can be placed in other programs to save more development time and provide quality material.

However, particularly back when video was king, a number of trainers got in trouble for using pieces of video from vendors' programs in different classroom environments, sometimes mixing video pieces from two or three different vendor programs to create entirely new courses. In today's DVD world this is both easier and harder to do, so be careful. The best approach is to explain to your vendor what you plan to do with the material and to ask how much leeway you have to make changes. If you are dissatisfied with the answer, negotiate a price for an "all uses" license, or find another more understanding vendor. Before you sign on the dotted line, know what your contract permits and doesn't permit you to do with the course materials you're planning to purchase.

PREPARING INSTRUCTORS AS A RAPID DEVELOPMENT TECHNIQUE

Another entire facet of rapid classroom development techniques relates to preparing the course instructors. Some might say this isn't development, but rather falls under the implementation phase. Possibly so, but you can't implement a class until the instructors are trained, so for the sake of argument, and because it's a good topic with lots of possible rapid development shortcuts, we'll discuss it here in development.

The most important rapid development technique related to instructor preparation has already been discussed; Be sure that your instructor guide matches the level of detail needed by your instructors. This alone means that you will spend less time on train-the-trainer processes and that your instructors will make fewer mistakes in following the lessons you've developed.

You can also save considerable travel time (not to mention wear and tear) by doing your instructor preparation long distance rather than bringing all your instructors to one location, either using the web or a simple telephone conference. This technique also requires a properly developed instructor guide, as well as instructors who know their business. It is not effective if your instructors are new to the process of instruction and need training not only on the program, but on facilitation skills as well. While not directly a rapid development technique, preparing your instructors long distance so to speak will save you time that you can then spend doing more and better development.

There is a rapid development technique that I have used effectively with less experienced instructors in situations in which I could not bring them together. I simply ask them to videotape themselves facilitating the class I developed and they were to teach (in a simulated setting naturally), and then have them send me a copy. After I view it, we have a phone conversation during which we view the tape together (a little cumbersome, but it works) and discuss their strengths and weaknesses in facilitation skills and content knowledge as they pertain specifically to the fairly detailed instructor guide I developed and the class they will be facilitating.

You can make this concept somewhat less cumbersome by using web meeting tools or synchronous delivery software if you have them, but the process itself remains the same.

This methodology was particularly useful in one case when I was working with instructors who had very limited experience in using the types of simulations I had developed for a particular class, but whom I could not bring together for a train-the-trainer session due to scheduling problems and other corporate exigencies. Using their videos I was able to see where they were having problems facilitating the simulations, and I actually revised a portion of the instructor guide based on those observations and our phone discussions. I admit that doing the revision cost me some development time, but it was well worth it, and certainly not as time-intensive as traveling to each location and working with them singularly.

I suppose this technique might work for general facilitation skills with brand new instructors as well, although I have never had the opportunity to try it. If you ever do have such an opportunity, let me know how it worked . . . or didn't.

Another rapid development technique for preparing instructors is to simply purchase your instructors. You can do this as part of a package when you buy a vendor's off-the-shelf product, as part of a contract when you have a consulting group develop a custom classroom program for you, or you can simply go out and hire seasoned, professional instructors to teach your program.

Whatever way you may do it, it will decrease your instructor preparation time and often be more cost-effective, as you did not have to spend the money bringing your own instructors up-to-speed on the program. And if you choose the right instructors, it will probably produce a more effective learning experience for your participants as well.

MEDIA RAPID DEVELOPMENT TECHNIQUES

Developing media for a face-to-face classroom program used to be one of the most time-consuming aspects of the entire process. The advent of computer projectors and PowerPoint slides has changed that considerably, some for the better, some not so. We've discussed PowerPoint as a rapid development technique earlier, but not as a process with its own rapid development shortcuts, so let's take a look at a few of these.

Rapid Development Techniques for PowerPoint

The first and simplest is to use templates. Creating a PowerPoint slide or series from scratch every time you develop a new classroom program can be a significant waste of time. Decide what you like and don't like in a PowerPoint slide, and then create a model (or two or three). Each time you develop a slide, use one of your models as your basis. You can even buy pre-made templates from vendors so you don't need to think about your slide style at all.

Next, stay away from animations and other "cute" techniques unless they specifically enhance the learning. These things take time, sometimes lots of time, time that can be better spent developing things that matter, even if they aren't as much fun.

By now most of your learners have seen what can be done with PowerPoint graphics and animations in a dozen presentations, so it's not a novel attention-getter (and if you need it as such, there is likely something much deeper wrong with your class). So stick to good, thoughtfully developed slides that help augment the learning, and save the bells and whistles to impress your audience when you are giving a speech at the local Rotary, not developing a classroom learning experience.

That's not to say that all animation is bad. Flow diagrams that show movement in a system or working diagrams of a cut-away machine functioning can enhance learning significantly, and, of course, builds always work well, but cartoon characters running across the screen for no real reason should be left to Disney or Pixar.

Which brings up the clip art characters that are now so prevalent in PowerPoint slides. Once again, if they don't enhance the learning, don't spend your time looking for them and adding them to your slides. At best they are likely to be boring, as your learners have seen them before, and at worst they can distract from the message your slide is trying to convey, a real disaster in a learning process!

The same goes for the complex graphics that you often see in medical or high-level manufacturing training. These take plenty of development time, and on a PowerPoint, no matter how large you project them, they are often unreadable. Complex graphics are for the participant package, in hard copy, where at worst your learners can pull out a magnifying glass to read them.

The Participant Package Revisited

The participant package is also a form of media, and a very important one. We've covered most of the rapid development shortcuts related to participant packages earlier, but here are a couple of reminders and maybe a new one or two.

- Use books, papers, and articles in your participant package in lieu of creating new material, but watch your copyright rights.

- If your learners have computers available, use websites that they can go to for material instead of putting it in your participant package. This requires good directions, not only to navigate to the right site, but also to navigate at the site to the things you want them to consider. It also requires constant surveillance that the sites are still there and haven't been changed, but can be well worth the trouble, particularly when the content requires a lot of revising or you want the learners to have the most up-to-date material.

- Create templates for the various types of materials you may put into a participant package.

- Keep names and phone numbers out of your participant package so you don't need to revise it continuously. If you need names, numbers, email addresses, etc., develop a pass-out, or better yet, put it online.

Flip Charts As a Rapid Development Technique

In classroom deliveries, flip charts used to be king. PowerPoint slides have now taken over that title, but flip charts are still very useful and can be a rapid development technique all by themselves. Using flip charts as an interactive learning tool allows the learner to become more a part of the learning process, providing information that you as the developer do not have to generate for your instructor guide or participant package. Flip charts are also easier to develop than basic informational slides, and they can be changed or even created on the fly, allowing the instructor to bring more learner-provided information to the forefront of a class discussion.

As a class discussion tool, they are much more versatile than PowerPoint slides, and they are often a nice change of pace as well. We are getting a little away from rapid development techniques here, but I wanted to impress on you the uses of this media format and the fact that using it in lieu of more formalized lectures or activities can be just as effective and save you plenty of development time. Here are some thoughts on creating and using flip charts that can help make them a rapid development shortcut for you.

Flip-Chart Thoughts
- Prepare complicated flip charts in advance.
- Ten lines per page is a maximum.
- Don't use the bottom third of the flip chart, as those in the back may not be able to see it.
- Write key points only.
- Title each page.
- Leave blank pages between prepared sheets.
- Use multiple colors, but use them systematically (red for emphasis, blue for key points, green for sub-points, and so on).

Rapid Development Techniques for Video

For the most part when we think of video today, we think of its use in web-based processes, but it is still a viable medium in the classroom as well. It is not a rapid development technique, however, as it takes time and considerable effort to produce. But there are a few rapid development techniques that you can use when you have decided to develop video for a face-to-face class.

- *Use off-the-shelf video and edit it.* We've discussed this before, although not specifically about video. It will save you immense amounts of time developing video for some aspect of classroom content if you can find a piece that works and has already been produced, or is close enough that you can retool it. Once again, be careful of your rights concerning making those changes you want to make in relation to the producer's copyright.

- *Use video slugs.* Creating a full video that is the basis for a class is a daunting task. Instead, develop video pieces (what are often called slugs) that enhance certain aspects of the class. This will decrease your development time considerably, and make the class more lively, as you can build other activities around the slugs.

- *Develop all your videos in discrete slugs.* Even if you are developing a longer video program, produce it in pieces so that if something changes you will only need to revise the piece that contains the change and not the entire program, saving you hours of revision time.

- *Combine your scripts and storyboards.* Video productions usually begin with the production of a scrip, followed by the development of a storyboard. You can save some development time by doing both simultaneously. This may mean you need to do a few revisions as it all comes together, particularly during the shooting and in the editing room, but that should be only a small percentage of the time you save by not doing each separately.

- *Use rapid prototyping.* We've discussed rapid prototyping already, so let's just say that it works very well in video production.

- *Use professionals.* As with many technology development processes, using people who do it for a living will save you large amounts of development time and possibly money as well, in the long run. There are a number of highly specialized jobs required for good video production, and the best development product will come from people who really know how to do them.

- *Don't be afraid of non-professional-looking videos.* This used to be a major consideration, as the common wisdom was that people were so used to professional video from television that less-than-perfect programs would turn them off. I'm not sure that was ever true, but it certainly is not today. There are TV programs and even movies that strive for an unfinished look, and the growth of web-based homemade video has been so overwhelming that perfect video quality is no longer paramount, and often not even a requirement.

One of my favorite rapid development techniques for video is to tape a subject-matter expert performing a task or a supervisor holding a meeting, then edit it down to key points and use it in class. It's not professional video, but as noted above, that's not necessarily important, and it does reduce development time by days and weeks.

One caveat here: while taking video of live processes can work very well, using non-professional actors in rehearsed (or even unrehearsed) simulation type situations does not. This is simply too non-professional for most learners to be comfortable with. If you are not taping real-life situations, go with professional video or none at all.

Other Classroom Media Rapid Development Techniques

There are a few other classroom media rapid development techniques that might be helpful to you in specific situations:

- Use audio recording of meetings, announcements, or other corporate communications instead of creating print material on the topic. Edit the recordings and augment them with questions to be answered or discussed to create an activity.

- Make your media easy to revise by using popular software like Word and PowerPoint, and not specialized software that others may not have or know how to use. Make it still easier to revise by keeping it simple.

- If still images are required for your material, consider taking pictures using a digital camera or perhaps purchasing an image library. Many of these libraries also have diagrams and cut-away models if you need them as well.

Face-to-face classroom programs have been around for a long time and are still one of the most prevalent forms of training delivery. As such, there are many rapid development techniques that have been tried to make the development of the materials required for a classroom faster and easier. You can't use them all at the same time, but as you develop, pick the ones that you think will work best in your situation and give them a try.

Chapter 3

Rapid On-the-Job Training Development

Entry and Exit for Development

- Begin with validated objectives, or at least a subject-matter expert who can help you write them as you develop the material
- End with an observation of a subject-matter expert using your material to do an on the job training program followed by revision if necessary

End Products

- Trainer Guide
- OJT Learning Guide
- Equipment List
- Performance Checklists

$\mathbf{A}$s mentioned previously, on-the-job training or OJT is itself a rapid development technique, as using it reduces the need for both learning materials and instructor preparation. That is, if the delivery of training through an on-the-job training process is developed properly. Unfortunately, too many organizations consider on-the-job training as simply saying to a subject-matter expert, "Hey, go teach this new person what you know." There is no denying that this is a rapid way to do training, or that in a vast majority of cases it is about as ineffective as it is fast.

The on-the-job training we will be discussing here is a structured learning experience in which the instructor is an SME, but one who has been trained on how to train and possibly certified as a content knowledge expert as well. It is most often done one-on-one and on the job site. This isn't an all-inclusive definition of OJT, as sometimes there are two or more trainees per instructor; and through the use of simulators, computers, and virtual reality systems, it might not even be done on the job site in all cases. However, for our purposes let's stick to the primary definition as given above.

In structured on-the-job training, there are four basic end products to the development process, a trainer guide, an OJT learning guide, equipment/simulators, and performance checklists. If this sounds a bit like a set of classroom materials to you, then give yourself a gold star. The difference is that in on-the-job training each of these items can be much less complex, and that's where rapid development comes in.

Here is an OJT development template that by itself is a good rapid development shortcut for creating OJT programs.

I. Materials

II. Objective(s)

III. Prepare trainee

    A. Purpose of session

    B. How session will be conducted

    C. Problems others have had

    D. Evaluation

    E. Any questions

IV. Key learning points

V. Expected results

VI. Work standards

VII. Sequence of activities

VIII. Demonstration

IX. Observation of trainee performance

X. Evaluation

TRAINER GUIDE

Let's take the trainer guide. You already know the trainer is going to be an SME; that's what on the job training is all about. Therefore, the trainer guide needs very little in the way of content information. Your objectives from the design phase, maybe a topic outline that you developed then as well, and perhaps a few notes on things to stress or go lightly on should be enough. You might want to add in the performance checklists that the instructor will use to determine mastery (don't forget the correct answers) and any directions for how to use the equipment or hold simulations that you think might be necessary, but if your OJT trainer is a true SME, even these can be minimal.

Your trainer training can also be simple. Content can be covered very quickly with a brief review of the objectives (the trainers in all likelihood know more than you do about it). Even trainer skills are minimal, as we are not talking about leading a classroom here, but rather working one-on-one with a singular individual. There are some specialized skills involved when instructing one-on-one though, and you'll probably want to do a little trainer analysis, then perhaps a bit of skills training to get all of your on-the-job training instructors up-to-speed. However, these skills are certainly fewer and easier to master than a complete set of classroom facilitation skills. Here is a list of some one-to-one skills you may want to work on with your OJT trainers

One-on-One Trainer Characteristics and Skills

- Has in-depth knowledge of content
- Exhibits confidence in self and the process being taught
- Is credible
- Follows the trainer guide
- Explains well
- Understands the basics of how adults learn
- Develops rapport with the trainee
- Involves the trainee in the training
- Can read body language
- Exhibits proper body language
- Makes good eye contact
- Listens well
- Is receptive to trainee's ideas
- Checks for understanding with questions and by repeating trainee comments

- Asks good questions and waits for answers
- Is patient
- Is flexible
- Has no annoying verbal or non-verbal habits
- Smiles

OJT LEARNING GUIDE

As most of what is done in on-the-job training is

> Tell me
>
> Show me
>
> Let me do

or with a bit more structure:

> Tell them
>
> Show them(in pieces)
>
> Do it for them (as a whole)
>
> *then have them*
>
> Tell you
>
> Show you
>
> Do it for themselves(practice)

then

> Do it for you to evaluate

the learning guide should also be rather slim, mostly objectives with space for notes and the performance checklists that will be used for evaluation (which also make for good retention tools). Activities in on-the-job training are usually the job performances. There is little need for long write-ups about these, as your OJT trainers should know them inside out, further decreasing the size of your learning guide compared to a classroom participant package.

If the performances are complicated, the learning guides might include references to operating and tech manuals, or actual parts of the manuals themselves if they're not too unwieldy. Referring to the manuals, the figures and diagrams they contain, or excerpts from them, will shorten your OJT learning guide development time and save you the burden of basically rewriting them to include the materials the trainees need for the on-the-job training.

In a really time-constrained on-the-job training development situation, you might even use the entire manual or whatever documentation you have on hand as the learning guide. In such a case you will need to give the OJT instructor specific directions in the trainer guide as to what part of the manual should be used with which objective and how to incorporate the practices, quizzes, etc., that you develop into the training. I don't recommend using tech manuals or even procedure manuals as the learning guide except in the direst of circumstances, as big, thick manuals tend to scare learners, or at least put them off. However, if done right, it can work and be a good rapid development technique for quickly creating a learning guide for OJT when you have few other choices.

EQUIPMENT AND SIMULATIONS AS RAPID DEVELOPMENT TECHNIQUES

A rapid on-the-job training development technique that I've found useful, particularly when current equipment is being used 24/7 for production, is to obtain old or outdated equipment that is still relatively close to that being used at present for training and to allow the subject-matter expert to explain what the differences are as part of the demonstration aspect of the OJT. Trainees can then practice on the old equipment with the on-the-job training instructor watching over their shoulders to make sure they grasp the difference between these machines and the ones they will actually work with. This will save you a lot of development time spent creating simulations, videos, or other less effective alternative learning processes and give the trainees a better hands-on experience as well.

I do some work for a vending company that uses this approach, actually creating a training laboratory full of this outdated equipment that is still good for training. This saves a lot of time waiting for the current equipment to become available, developing materials that take the place of the actual machines, or, in the case of my vending company client, traveling to their clients' locations to train new technicians.

Another type of on-the-job training rapid development technique is to use modern technology as part of your OJT, such as computer-based simulations and even virtual reality. On the surface these would not seem to be rapid development shortcuts, as they take considerable time to develop, but, as we'll discuss later, these high-tech processes are wonderfully versatile and can be repurposed in part or in whole for a variety of uses. Depending on the percent of equipment use in your on-the-job training environment and the number of different but related training needs you have that might include a particular piece of equipment, they can be real time savers over the long term.

THE SUBJECT-MATTER EXPERT AS AN OJT RAPID DEVELOPMENT TECHNIQUE

An excellent rapid development technique for on-the-job training is to use your subject-matter experts for more than just instruction. Because these are the people who will be facilitating the training, you might ask for their thoughts on how they would teach the content and what materials they would use before you begin to develop. They may even have materials available in their own files for you to borrow that can shortcut your material development even further.

A more elegant way to use your subject-matter experts is to provide them with a simple content outline and then observe them while they teach it, using their ideas and approaches to complete the development of your own on-the-job training materials. If you want to be even more elegant, after you've created the materials, have the same subject-matter experts teach again, using your materials in a live pilot situation, then make final revisions based on what you observed and/or discussed with your subject-matter expert.

By the way, this rapid development technique is also usable in classroom deliveries when your instructors are subject-matter experts. It works better with fewer instructors, and is a bit like the trainer-based development we talked about earlier, but in this case we are using the expertise of the trainer/SME to provide the information for the scaled-down instructor guide and even the participant package materials and media, rather than the more limited knowledge of the developer.

One final thought, if you have a number of OJT trainers training on the same process in different locations, have them observe your expert doing the training with your materials as part of their train-the-trainer process. Be sure they have a copy of the materials, as well, to follow along and for note-taking.

If you can't bring them together as a group for this observation, use video again. Teamed with a simple conference call with the expert SME to discuss what they observed on the video, this can be a very effective and time-saving RDT.

Here are some hints for working with SMEs that you might find helpful.

- When requesting an SME from a department, provide the manager with a list of the characteristics you are looking for.

- Prepare your SME with a list of topics or concepts you want to cover, and even objectives and test questions if you have them.

- Listen, don't talk.

- Ask good follow-up questions.

- Don't interrupt to ask a new questions until the SME's thought is complete.

- When you move from general questions to specific questions, give the SME a chance to make the mental change.

- Don't use trainer terminology like *job aids* or *performance tools*. Ask it in their language, or they won't know what you are looking for.

- Use both verbal (ahh, uh-huh) and nonverbal (smiling, nodding, frowning, open body language, eye contact) behaviors to elicit more and better responses.

- Be careful not to ask multiple questions at the same time. Keep it simple to get solid answers.

- Keep your SMEs updated on the progress of the course, as they own part of it now. This will pay big dividends later when you need reviewers.

- When you have follow-up questions, instead of another meeting or even an e-mail, try posting them on the corporate intranet to get other SMEs interested.

Chapter 4

Rapid Asynchronous e-Learning Course Development

Entry and Exit for Development
- Begin with validated objectives and an expanded outline, both of which have been reviewed and signed off on by appropriate subject-matter experts and stakeholders.
- End with a piloted and revised program that is ready for distribution

End Products
- Detailed Outline
- Script
- Storyboard
- Graphics
- Animations
- Video
- Programmed Learning Intervention in Correct Delivery Mode
- Learner Evaluation Instruments and/or Questions
- Supporting Documentation and Training for New Users

. . . . Asynchronous e-learning, that is e-learning that is self instructional in nature, is probably the most demanding of the major training delivery systems as far as materials development is concerned. It requires succinctly written objectives, a large number of learner evaluation questions, very detailed outlines, scripts, storyboards, programming, graphics, animations, video, activities, and rigorous beta tests and piloting. However, this complexity lends itself to many chances for rapid development shortcuts as well.

You may ask yourself, "Well, if the development is that complicated, why use this type of delivery at all?" Why indeed! From the early days of the CBT "electronic page turners" right up to today's web-based "read and/or listen to some screens, get asked a question or two, read and/or listen to some more screens, take the test" compliance training modules, trainers have been putting out a lot of really bad asynchronous e-learning under a variety of labels, mostly because they haven't taken the time, or never had the time, to do it properly.

The important thing to remember with this type of delivery is that it does take a powerful amount of development, so the answer to your question is that you'd better have a really good reason for using it. Here is a list of do's and don'ts to consider when you are thinking about using an asynchronous delivery, followed by a list of its advantages that may help answer the question, "Why?".

Do's for Asynchronous e-Learning

- Use quick start guides to help your learners hit the ground running.
- Run focus groups ahead of time to determine learner needs and build excitement.
- Have a pop-up support function available inside your programs.
- Make sure your start-up phone-in support is 24/7 for the first few weeks.
- Create help screens in your program introduction.
- Have a help desk number available as a menu pop-up.
- Create a major launch event that goes throughout the organization.
- Use giveaways to remind the learners about e-learning.
- Use personal contact where possible.
- Step up your marketing to all levels.
- Use e-mail to announce new programs.
- Communicate learner and departmental successes.

- Write reports and send them to all interested parties.
- Develop rewards and incentives for learners and supervisors:
  - Produce printable completion certificates that can be exchanged for prizes.
  - For management development and other multi-program processes, create a wall display plaque with spaces for stickers as programs are completed.
  - When a program is completed, have a copy of the completion certificate sent to the learner's boss's printer or computer.
  - Create a culture that prizes learning.
  - Find incentives for sharing what learners learned with others.
- Develop peer recognition processes:
  - Name a learner of the month.
  - Create special events.
  - Send group e-mails.
  - Institute learner chat rooms or electronic bulletin boards.
  - Send out e-news letters.

Advantages of Asynchronous e-learning

- Cost savings (be careful to consider hardware costs if necessary)
- More effective delivery of content
- Greater learner choice
- Greater manager control
- Reduced training time
- Geographically neutral
- Allows learning 24/7
- Easily updateable
- Provides a consistent message
- Trains large numbers in a short time
- Learners move at own pace
- Reduces travel expenses
- More time-effective for instructors
- Enhances self-direction

RAPID PROTOTYPING REDUX

If you do decide that asynchronous e-learning is the most effective delivery process for your training need and environment, you will want to do all you can to make the development faster. One of the most effective ways is a concept we have already discussed, rapid prototyping. Rapid prototyping was created for asynchronous e-learning, and it probably works best for this type of delivery. Whether you choose the build a complete piece method, build a working model design, the simple static graphics demonstration, some combination of the three, or your own conceptualization, rapid prototyping can quickly stop you from going down the wrong development path before you are too far along to make time- and cost-efficient changes. Rapid prototyping will also keep you out of the "blame game" that often occurs at the end of an asynchronous development when the client or stakeholder sees a finished product that was not at all what he visualized when you had your first meeting. This saves not only time and money, but reputations as well.

CONSULTANTS AS AN ASYNCHRONOUS RAPID DEVELOPMENT TECHNIQUE

Perhaps an even more rapid development technique than rapid prototyping is using a consultant to assist you in your asynchronous development. This has a great number of advantages, not the least of which is that the right consultant has more resources than you do, so she can develop your asynchronous material faster. If you find the right one he or she will have an entire team, including writers, programmers, graphics artists, video specialists, etc., to work on your project. Each of these experts will be able to do his or her part of the development much faster than your internal training resources will, unless you have the same type of staff internally, and they have nothing else to do but work on your program.

This last comment is much more important than it might seem at first. I had an experience working for a large organization that did have graphic artists, programmers, and a video production group. However, none of these resources worked directly for training. I was informed that if I provided these internal resources with a script and storyboard for the asynchronous program the training department had hired me to develop, they could handle the rest, with a little monitoring, naturally. This may have been true, but they were also doing marketing stuff, merchandising stuff, public relations stuff, speeches for the CEO and the other "Os," and, of course, each of these customers wanted their stuff yesterday, just like me. In the end, to get the training done on time we actually had to go out to a multi-media development group anyway, but we wasted many precious days in waiting for the internal folks to produce before we figured this out, and then more time in looking for and getting on the schedule of a good multi-media shop.

The right asynchronous consulting group will also likely have more experience than you and your group in developing the various pieces of an asynchronous development, as this is what they do for a living. Therefore, they will be more efficient in the use of their own time. This experience itself is a rapid development shortcut.

Choosing a Consultant

Considerations When Evaluating an Asynchronous Consultant
General

1. What is the background and credentials of the principals?
2. Does their facility have the necessary technology?
3. What are their normal deliverables to a client?
4. Do they have any experience in developing administration or support processes for clients?
5. What common problems do they encounter when working with their clients?

Statistics

6. How many asynchronous training programs have they completed?
7. Of these, how many have high-level/mid-level interactivity?
8. What do they consider to be a proper range of development hours to completed minutes of instruction for programs with:

    High interactivity

    Mid-level interactivity

    Low-level interactivity

9. What is their estimated cost per hour for:

    Instructional designers

    Graphic designers

    Programmers

    Video production

    Video editing

Program Quality

10. Do their sample programs have objectives that are used to guide the participants throughout the learning?

11. Do their sample programs include self-quizzes that are related to the objectives?

12. Have they used multiple response questioning?

13. Do they have good directions and other appropriate front matter in their programs?

14. Are their user interfaces easy to use and creative?

15. Are their programs easy to navigate through?

Interaction

16. Do they have examples of their use of high-level simulations?

17. Do they have examples of their use of branching techniques, both for questions and for content?

18. Do they have examples of their use of rollover's and links to both program internal and external resources?

Capabilities

19. Who is on their permanent staff? What are their credentials and experience?

20. Who does the cover:

    Designing

    Script writing

    Graphics

    Animation

    Programming

    Videography

    Editing

    Sound

    General producing

    Project management

21. What are their in-house video capabilities?

22. What authoring systems do they use/recommend?

23. What is their experience with web-based delivery?

    Software used?

    Streaming audio and video?

24. What are their audio capabilities?

    Narration

    Do they have examples of multiple narration or special audio effects?

Miscellaneous

25. Do they know anything about:

    Rapid prototyping

    Object-oriented learning

As the above list of questions indicates, there are a great many things you need to think about when choosing a consultant to help you do part or all of rapid asynchronous course development. Some of these considerations are the same as for any type of training vendor: history, customer service, samples of work, customer endorsements. However, here are some aspects that take on more significance when the consultant is doing asynchronous development.

First, be sure you choose a group who specializes in creating training programs. Early on in the growth cycle of e-learning, many software and computer companies saw that developing computer-based training programs could be a possible revenue stream. They touted their ability to do so, even when they had little or no experience, simply because they "knew" computers. This isn't as prevalent today, but it does still occur. If you want rapid development, you need a consulting group who knows not just computers, but training programs as well, and knows how to do them not only fast, but right.

Look for a group with a full-time or consistent part-time staff. Asynchronous development is a team effort with a lot of cross-talk and synergy needed among the team members. A consulting group with full-time programmers, graphic artists, and developers will have that synergy and can develop your program faster and better. A consulting firm that hires staff on an as-needed basis may not. Ask groups under consideration for information on part-time and full-time staff, and who exactly will be working on your project. Having a great full-time staff, but being so busy that they need to hire part-timers for your project is of little value to you.

Big Versus Small

That being said, smaller can often be better. In most big cities and larger towns there will be one or two local "shops" that have and can develop asynchronous programs. You don't necessarily need to go to the large national development houses to do a program. You will need to vet these smaller vendors more carefully, for the reasons we've already mentioned, but they will be more convenient, perhaps be more responsive to your needs, and may charge less for the same quality product. Be careful though that your project doesn't overwhelm their resources and that they have the time to get it done on time.

Local shop or nationwide development house, a consultant can be an excellent rapid development technique for your asynchronous program, not to mention a way to develop a more effective program. Experienced vendors will know what works in an asynchronous delivery and what doesn't, and what could work if you allow them a little leeway.

Working with a Consultant

But not too much leeway, as the good ones are usually staffed with very creative people, sometimes too creative. They can lose track of the fact that this is a training program, not an entertainment package, and overload your design with "neat" things that don't necessarily contribute to the learning—and neat things take more time.

When you are working with a consulting group, make your development more rapid by giving them something to work with in the beginning. I've seen time-harassed trainers who hire a consultant and simply say, "This is kind of what I'm looking for. Show me what you can do." This isn't the wrong approach, as good consultants can overcome a lack of direction by asking the right questions and drawing what they require from you as the development progresses, but it certainly will not lend itself to rapid course development, as the consultants will need to learn more about your training need, your company, your trainees, and many other things you already know before they can begin development.

Make their part of your project more efficient by giving them all the background knowledge, direction, and even possible ideas for activities or format that you can before they start. I prefer to provide my asynchronous consulting group with a preliminary script and really rudimentary storyboard for an asynchronous development. I even give them some thoughts on activities I'd like to see, although most of these are usually too grandiose for my time and/or budget and usually end up being scaled down or changed by my experienced consulting partners.

However, my briefing and semi-developed plans allow them to focus on what they do best, translating my concepts into an effective asynchronous program, rather than doing design and early development work that I can do more effectively, as I know my organization, my learners, and the general way I need the program to work.

Now you might say, "If I'm going to do the analysis, write the objectives, create the evaluations, and develop a script and storyboard myself, what do I need a consultant for?" and in most deliveries you'd be right. But asynchronous e-learning is a different animal, as we have already noted, and doing all of that isn't even half of the work of developing a good program. The half an asynchronous consulting group will do for you can be the most time-consuming aspect of all the instructional design phases, and so well worth thinking about outsourcing.

When working with consulting groups in asynchronous developments, you also need to monitor them rather closely to keep your rapid development rapid. The best approach is to have the project manager (they should assign you one) create a project plan with milestones, review sessions, and delivery dates. In most cases the milestones will be related to the deliverables as outlined in your contract with them, but you may want interim milestones as well, depending on the size and complexity of your project.

You can also add rapid prototyping milestones and any other logical review points that make sense to the project plan (which they should also create for you.) This way you can monitor progress and make sure things are coming together the way you and the consultant envisioned.

These milestone meetings should take very little of your time, another rapid development shortcut, and can be done telephonically if your consultant is not local. However, they are critical. One week with your consultant going off-track can wipe out all of the rapid development gains you might have achieved for the entire program.

Don't emulate a colleague of mine from back in the early days of e-learning who knew he knew nothing about how to do it, but knew he wanted it, so he hired a nationally recognized consulting group to "create" an e-learning based first-level supervisory skills program for his organization, a "turnkey operation," as the consultant called it. He got it too, a wonderful program, on time, on budget, and at the perfect level . . . for his top managers. A little monitoring, even if he didn't understand the intricacies of e-learning, would quickly have caught the level creep and brought the consultant back to the right altitude for his supervisors.

Cost

Speaking of budget, of course the biggest drawback to using a consulting group for your rapid asynchronous development is usually the cost. There are consultants, and then there are consultants, and you can usually find a development shop somewhere who will develop to your budget, in which case you will get what your budget pays for. The old adage, "You can have it cheap, fast, or good, or any two of these, but not all three," pertains perfectly to asynchronous development. If you want it rapid and good, you have to pay the price. If you are hoping for anything else, I suggest you go back to the design phase and revisit your decision to use an asynchronous delivery system to begin with.

Do your cost/benefit analysis, consider what you need by when, and if the numbers come out right, search out an experienced asynchronous consultant who can develop what you need within the time and cost that you need it. Anything else will in the end never be a truly rapid asynchronous development technique.

BUYING COMPLETE OFF-THE-SHELF PACKAGES AS A RAPID DEVELOPMENT TECHNIQUE

There are a couple of other rapid development techniques for asynchronous development that involve vendors. The first of these is to simply buy a vendor-created off-the-shelf asynchronous program. There are many out there, and the time you spend finding the one that matches your development needs will almost certainly be less than the time you spend developing your own, or having someone else do a custom development for you. Use your objectives as your guide in choosing the right program, and do a cost/benefit analysis to make sure this is a logical approach.

You also need to know something about the vendor you are buying a program from and the contractual restrictions on the use of their programs from any vendor you are considering, the former not being as important here as it was when you were choosing a vendor to actually develop for you, the latter being more so as your cost/benefit analysis should not only consider initial costs but continuing costs as well.

One other thought in this area: Be sure the vendor program can run on your learning management system. If you don't know what this means, or simply want more information on learning management systems, you might want to go to the Asynchronous e-Learning chapter of *Rapid Instructional Design* or any of the e-learning books in the suggested reading list.

Here is a series of questions from *Rapid Instructional Design* that you might want to ask to help you determine whether an off-the-shelf asynchronous package may be the right rapid development shortcut for you.

Questions to Ask Before Purchasing an Off-the-Shelf Asynchronous Program

- Do the strengths of program match the content you must deliver?

- Do the delivery processes match our learning environment?

- Will this program save us design, development, and/or implementation time?

- Will it be efficient for our learners?

- Overall, will it provide us with any real cost savings?

- Will our culture support the program's learning environment?

- Do we have the technology infrastructure in place to support the program?

- Do we have the funding to purchase it?

- Will we be able to support and maintain the program under current or future conditions?

- Is there visible high-level support for the program's content?

- Are our learners comfortable with operating the technology required by the program?

CUSTOMIZING VENDOR OFF-THE-SHELF PACKAGES AS A RAPID DEVELOPMENT TECHNIQUE

If you can't find an off-the-shelf program the fits your objectives closely enough, you may be able to customize one. We talked about this a bit in the chapter on rapid classroom development, but you are likely to get more for your time and money using this rapid development technique in asynchronous development.

There are a number of vendors out there who will customize their asynchronous programs to meet your particular training needs, even going so far as to redo objectives and sequencing. Don't get this confused with the so-called customization that basically consists of adding your company name and logo to the program. If you want true rapid development, you need to find a vendor willing to do much more than that. Some who claim to have a customizable product won't even consider changing an objective or simulation for you.

You might also be able to convince the vendor to allow you or your staff to customize their program. This is more difficult to negotiate, and can be a lot more difficult to do if you do not have the expertise in your group. However, if you can convince the vendor that the integrity of their program will not be compromised (there is some pride of authorship here, too) and you have the ability, customizing an off-the-shelf program yourself can save you much development time and some dollars.

BUYING ASYNCHRONOUS ACTIVITIES AS A RAPID DEVELOPMENT TECHNIQUE

Another vendor-based rapid development technique for asynchronous development is to hire an experienced consultant to create the asynchronous activities you require for your program. As we mentioned earlier, asynchronous activities are the most time-consuming of development processes, so hiring a consultant just for this purpose can really decrease your development time without busting your budget. You might also consider hiring a scriptwriter specifically to write your scripts or a graphics artist to create your graphics. Again, if you and your staff don't have these types of expertise, this can be a very effective rapid development technique.

There are vendors who create asynchronous activities for sale as well, just as they do classroom activities, although not a great number of them. You have a better chance finding an activity or two that a vendor used in their own programs, and asking whether you can purchase it for reuse. This type of request is not common, but a good developer looks for rapid shortcuts wherever they can be found. You'll probably need to explain in detail what you want and how you'll use it and to sign all sorts of copyright and usage agreements, but it may be worth it. There are also compatibility issues, not only internal to your program, but external to your learning management system as well. These can usually be worked out, and in my experience vendors are much more comfortable selling a piece of a program for another purpose than allowing someone to "mess" with their whole program.

SCRIPTS AND STORYBOARDS

Beyond vendors and rapid prototyping, there are a number of more specific things you can do to make your development of an asynchronous program more rapid. Some of these are related to your script and storyboard development, and one of the basic rapid techniques here is simply to do them. Many developers who are new to asynchronous development tend to skip these documents and go straight from an outline to creating the materials. This often leads to confusion, rework, and more revisions, all of which make the development less rapid.

When developing your scripts and storyboards, keeping them simple is the most rapid development technique I can think of. This isn't Hollywood, and you don't need to have a perfect scrip for your star actor to read or a storyboard that the director will be working from. I prefer a simple two-column format for the script, such as the one in Figure 4.1, and the addition of a third column to make it a storyboard, as shown in Figure 4.2. If you are doing the development yourself, this should be more than sufficient to keep you on track during development, and if you are using a consultant it will be a good place for him or her to start.

If you have a number of resources, internal and/or external, working on a series of asynchronous development projects at the same time, a good rapid development technique is to create a template for both your script and your storyboard that will be used by all your developers. This makes it easier for everyone to see at what stage the development is for any project and where the group is as a whole, in case resources have to be reallocated. It also makes it a heck of a lot easier on your programming and graphics people, as each script or storyboard they see has the same basic makeup as ones they have already worked with.

Here are some hints on script writing that can help speed up your asynchronous development, followed by an example (Figure 4.3) of a different type of storyboard template that is somewhat more suited to asynchronous development and might help you in designing your own rapid asynchronous development storyboard template.

Script Writing Hints

- Keep your sentences short.

- Use repetition.

- Remember to write for your audience, not for yourself.

- Write as you speak.

- Scripts must be short, and script pieces even shorter.

- Three items of information in each script piece is a good rule of thumb.
- Stay on message.
- Write when the time is best for you.
- Do openings, closings, and even transitions last.
- Plan for at least three drafts of anything you write.
- Listen to your reviewers.
- Define all technical terms.

Script Title: _____

Page: _____   Rev. _____

Content Outline	Script

Figure 4.1. Two-Column Script

Storyboard for _____

Page number _____ of _____ Revision Number: _____

Screen	Script	Visuals

Figure 4.2. Three-Column Storyboard

REPURPOSING CLASSROOM ACTIVITIES FOR ASYNCHRONOUS DEVELOPMENT

Creating asynchronous activities is one of the most time-consuming of development processes, as such activities require meticulous attention to detail and usually a lot of programming. So any way that you can find to develop them more rapidly is a big help. One of the most prevalent of rapid development techniques for asynchronous activities, although not necessarily the most effective, is to repurpose classroom activities that have already been developed for a stand-up class. This is, or at least has been, a common practice simply because of the number of trainers who have been trying to repurpose entire classroom programs into asynchronous deliveries.

It has also not been totally successful, as there are many activities used in the classroom that don't translate well to a self-instructional asynchronous environment where there are no other learners to interact with. The lack of a facilitator in such an environment restricts the use of classroom activities even more. The question, "Who is available to answer learner questions concerning the activity's directions

Project: _____ File Name: _____

Screen ID: _____ Last Date Saved: _____

Graphics	Text/Narration	
Actions/Navigation	**Sound**	**Notes**

Figure 4.3. Five-Part Asynchronous Storyboard

or during the activity itself?" has never been adequately answered in asynchronous learning.

That's not to say that you can't repurpose classroom activities as a rapid development technique. There are many classroom activities that do translate well to an asynchronous program. You just need to choose wisely, plan well, develop intricately, and pilot, pilot, pilot.

Obviously, group-based activities will not translate well, as there is no group when you are learning in a self-instructional mode, but question/answer activities translate very well, as do simulations that are not team based, particularly if you can have the computer play various roles. Role plays themselves can be repurposed, although it is much more difficult and certainly not as realistic. On the other hand, computers don't ad lib their roles as people tend to do. Games are usually a good candidate for translation to a synchronous environment, although the competition aspect becomes learner versus computer for the most part.

If you are attempting to repurpose an entire stand-up class into an asynchronous delivery, choose carefully the activities you will bring over and be prepared to create new ones as there are some that simply will not work.

A rapid development shortcut in these situations is to look at other similar stand-up classes that have different activities that may translate better, and use them instead of the ones from the original class. These classes might be your own, from someone else, or you may find repurposeable activities in the books and Pfeiffer *Annuals* we mentioned during our discussion of classroom activities.

REPURPOSING VIDEO SLUGS

You can also speed up your development of asynchronous programs by repurposing classroom videos. If the ones being used for the class currently are somewhat old, you may need to have them re-mastered in a digital format, and probably edited, but even small pieces of video can become the basis for effective learning modules in an asynchronous development when text screens and questions are built around them. They can also be used in the creation of examples and simulations.

The same holds true for videos that are not part of a current class. You'll need to reach an understanding with the copyright owner concerning how you plan to use them, but using excerpts from previously created videos in your asynchronous programs instead of developing your own can save you large amounts of development time and money.

A rapid development hint here, as we mentioned earlier, is to create all of your videos, classroom, asynchronous, etc., in small pieces, what we've referred to as video slugs. That way you can easily repurpose these slugs for any number of programs. It is also a simple method for making your videos more revision-friendly, as you may only need to revise one or two slugs and not an entire video program when something changes in the organization.

OTHER RAPID DEVELOPMENT TECHNIQUES FOR ASYNCHRONOUS DEVELOPMENT

Here are a few more miscellaneous but very useful hints to speed up the development of your asynchronous programs.

If you are creating a software application learning package for an asynchronous delivery, make full use of the software's tutorial and help functions. Instead of redeveloping the wheel, so to speak, refer the learners to various aspects of these functions for basic or in-depth knowledge, and even more importantly, to get them comfortable with using the functions. This will cut back the amount of original material you need to create significantly and make the learners more independent when they run into problems or forget what your program taught them.

As noted earlier, there are authoring tools with templates as well as entire authoring systems for use in developing asynchronous programs. It takes some time to learn them, and once you do you are kind of stuck with the one you chose, as it takes more time to learn another, but they can be great development shortcuts. The seasoned developer might find them a bit constricting, particularly as they require you to design using their methodology as well, but for new developers they can be a great help, and even seasoned developers can use the ideas and templates they present.

Other development tools that can function as asynchronous e-learning shortcuts include Macromedia Breeze, Articulate, SNAP!, and Studio. These are not authoring systems but software programs that work well in creating pieces of asynchronous learning and as such are often more flexible than a lock-step authoring system.

If you are really going out on your own, you can find collections of buttons and icons online, as well as background images and even motion graphics or animations that are for sale at reasonable prices to make your "from scratch" development faster.

When repurposing a classroom or even an on-the-job training program into an asynchronous delivery, be careful about overusing all the neat bells and whistles you now have available. Many developers become so enamored with adding these little "extras," simply because they can, that they either lose track of the learning process or simply run out of time and end up with a program that does not fulfill all the objectives. Bells and whistles are fine and fun, but don't forget why you are developing this thing in the first place.

Begin involving stakeholders and end-users in your development process from the start. Don't wait until the pilot to ask their opinions. We've discussed this concept from a number of directions, but it bears repeating. It wastes tremendous amounts of development time to be going down the wrong path, a path neither the stakeholders wanted nor the end-users can use effectively. Even developing an activity that doesn't fit their requirements can waste amazing amounts of time in an asynchronous development.

For example, I added a summary activity to an asynchronous program on problem solving once that was based on playing cards at a Las Vegas casino. It wasn't terribly critical to the learning, but it worked well, was fun, and took a significant amount of my time, a graphic artist's time, and of course a programmer's time to develop. When the stakeholder saw it (at the pilot) his comment was, "We don't want to teach gambling in our organization." I still have it in my activities file in case anyone is interested. This is another reason for rapid prototyping.

Use image libraries and take digital photos. We've mentioned this before as well, but it is an especially useful rapid development technique in asynchronous development. You need lots of graphics and visuals in asynchronous learning; it's a visual process, and your learners expect it. So look for places where you can obtain already developed ones, such as image libraries, or go out and shoot your own with a digital camera. Where they fit, photographs will be faster to develop than hand-drawn graphics, and they may even be a better learning aid under the right circumstances.

Beware of "scope creep" and "neat creep." Most asynchronous programs suffer from scope creep, that is, when someone, usually a stakeholder, decides somewhere along the line that "more" is needed for the program. A little of this can and should be expected, but holding it down to something rational will save you a lot of development time and polish up your collaboration skills as well.

Having a specifically worded, end-product-based contract and/or project plan that everyone agrees to in advance is one way to reduce scope creep. Another is to use rapid prototyping. Keeping stakeholders involved all during the development helps too, as does having review points with signoffs. You'll never stop scope creep entirely; it's part of the asynchronous process, and sometimes useful as you find content areas that were missed in the objectives. But you need to control it, or it will control your development.

"Neat creep" is my term for something we already mentioned, adding too many bells and whistles to the program. Neat creep occurs when the developer, the graphic artist, the programmer, or just about anybody on the development team adds something to the program because it's so "neat." This can be something as simple as an activity (my gambling activity from earlier is sort of an example of this) or an entire theme for a program. I once sat with a multi-media "expert" who had my client enamored over the concept of doing her entire asynchronous program with a "Star Wars" motif, music, sound effects, and all. It was "neat," no doubt about it, but it did little to enhance the learning of a series of new accounting procedures and would have taken us hundreds of hours of manipulation to make the content fit the theme, not to mention the hours of programming involved in getting the characters to walk and talk properly. In the end my client agreed with me, although sorrowfully. The program was developed in much less time, and worked just as well, but I have to admit it wasn't as much fun.

No matter what the level, neat creep costs you development time, time better spent creating materials that the learners can use to learn. Guarding against neat creep and scope creep are good rapid development techniques.

If you decide to develop a piece of asynchronous learning as a rapid development shortcut, or as part of a blended development, here is a checklist of things to do that can help you manage the process.

- Create a project management plan.
- Develop functional and visual prototypes.
- Create interaction and navigation models.
- Establish budget and time frame.
- Create a development plan for the project.
- Assign development team roles and responsibilities.
- Develop a goal statement.
- Isolate research and development requirements.
- Develop a communication plan.
- Develop a electronic file exchange system.
- Perform all necessary analysis and create analysis report.
- Sequence content.
- Select instructional methods.
- Create menu structure.
- Develop learner assessments.
- Create file-naming procedures.
- Develop standards for text, graphics audio, video, and animation elements.
- Develop artwork.
- Create implementation plan.
- Integrate content into program structures.

- Beta test.
- Pilot.
- Hold all required reviews.
- Create reproducible master or publish to net.
- Create follow-up plan.
- Create program evaluation plan.

Chapter 5

Rapid Synchronous e-Learning Course Development

Entry and Exit for Development
- Begin with validated objectives and a content outline, or in the case of repurposing from a classroom, a proper instructor guide and participant package with associated media.
- End with a complete synchronous program that has been piloted using both representative learners in a distance environment and a representative facilitator.

End Products
- Synchronous Instructor Guide
- Electronic and/or Hard Copy Participant Package
- Media Developed Specifically for Synchronous Instruction
- Activities Developed Specifically for Synchronous Instruction
- Synchronous Instructor's Train-the-Trainer Program
- Learner Evaluation Processes

Synchronous e-learning is a delivery system in which the instructor and the learners are in the learning environment at the same time, but instead of being physically together, as in a face-to-face classroom, they are connected and communicate by computer and phone line.

REPURPOSING STAND-UP CLASSES AS A SYNCHRONOUS RAPID DEVELOPMENT TECHNIQUE

When synchronous e-learning was first introduced, it was touted as being a rapid development technique all by itself. The hype was that you could take your current classroom programs and with practically no revisions magically change them into synchronous e-learning programs. These programs were just as effective, and didn't require your trainees or instructor to fly, drive, or otherwise travel to a training class. The same was true of instructors, or so it was said. A good classroom instructor could easily translate into a synchronous environment with almost no training or preparation at all.

The purpose of repurposing to synchronous instruction was obviously time and money savings, achieved by reduced travel costs and no longer needing to do the extensive material revisions that are required when repurposing a classroom program for an asynchronous delivery. Unfortunately, this promise wasn't, and still isn't, a reality.

There is much that can be used from a face-to-face class in a synchronous environment, particularly if the materials have been properly developed with good objectives and content outlines. However, the way activities function in a synchronous classroom and the skills required of the synchronous instructor are different enough to require a significant amount of development revision and instructor preparation. For example, a simple triad role play, which is a staple of classroom development, requires much more planning in an asynchronous environment and software that has multiple private chat room facilities, which some synchronous software does not. The debriefing is much longer and often becomes a question/answer session, as the usual free flow of ideas that is common in a face-to-face classroom does not work well in a synchronous environment.

A course syllabus is more important for a synchronous course, and both pre- and post-class structured communications between learners and facilitator is more critical as well.

The purpose of this book is not to consider these differences in any detail, nor to discuss how to design synchronous e-learning interventions. Both processes are explored at length in *Rapid Instructional Design* and other books. Just in case though, here is a summary list of various synchronous learning concepts that may help you understand the process just a little better before we talk about rapid development techniques for it.

Advantages of Synchronous e-Learning

- Efficient for a geographically dispersed audience
- Easily revised if content is unstable

- Efficient when delivery of content is limited to once or a few times
- Allows real-time access to an expert
- Effective when learner collaboration is important
- Useful when content requires a classroom type of delivery
- Can be developed quickly when design time is short but a distance learning delivery is required

Disadvantages of Synchronous e-Learning

General

- Requires proper software or technology
- May be ineffective due to lack of trained facilitators
- Requires learners to be prepared for a synchronous e-learning delivery
- Not effective when content requires face-to-face delivery
- Not efficient when the class needs to be run many times

For the Facilitator

- No eye contact
- No idea of what the learners are doing
- Learners can't use facilitator's visual cues
  - Body lean
  - Movement
  - Smiles
- Facilitator can't use learners' visual cues to speed up, slow down, go over again
- Voice is everything
- Positive reinforcement is difficult
- Not used to sending or receiving reinforcement via phone line
  - Emotions sound different on the phone

For the Learner

- No eye contact
- Multitasking allure
- No justification for participating

- No nonverbal instructor feedback
- Less verbal or nonverbal feedback from colleagues

Misconceptions Concerning Synchronous e-Learning

- Learners aren't comfortable with it.

    Sometimes they are more comfortable than in a classroom.

- There is less demand for an instructor's time.

    Depending on the design, it may take more instructor prep-aration and follow-up time, although they do not need to travel.

- Interactions are limited.

    Only by the instructional designer or facilitator's knowledge and creativity.

- There is less social interaction.

    Only if the instructional designer or facilitator allows this to happen through poor planning.

- Hundreds of learners can learn at once.

    They can be taught, but that has little to do with their learning.

All this doesn't mean that you can't repurpose your stand-up class-rooms for synchronous e-learning; it simply indicates that you'll need to carefully analyze the material available in your classroom programs, then do an in-depth determination of what you will be able to use and what you'll need to create for the new synchronous delivery.

Begin this process by considering the characteristics of your instructor-led classes. Do they have strong objectives? Are they heav-ily visual? Is there a lot of instructor-learner interaction? These are characteristics that lend themselves to synchronous deliveries.

Do they require a lot of group interaction? Are they more instructor-centric? Are there complex but critical activities? These are characteristics that make repurposing more difficult, not impos-sible, but they certainly lower the repurposing process's usefulness as a rapid development technique.

Repurposing classroom programs for synchronous e-learning can still be a very efficient rapid development technique, particularly if your company has reduced travel allowances and you're hoping to use synchronous software to hold classes that were once face-to-face meetings. Just remember that it ain't as easy as it might seem.

REPURPOSING CLASSROOM (AND OTHER) ACTIVITIES

We've discussed this concept before, and you should be getting the message by now that this is a key rapid development technique in many situations, but just in case . . .

You can speed up development of synchronous e-learning courses by repurposing classroom activities, even if you can't or don't want to repurpose an entire class. The activity doesn't even need to be part of a course that has similar content. It can be something that worked well from another course, particularly another synchronous course, or even an activity from a vendor, although vendor-created and sold activities for synchronous courses are still not very common.

One important caveat here though: Be sure you limit your synchronous activities to fifteen minutes or less. This isn't a classroom where the learners are basically captives. Activities that are too long can often lead to web browsing, e-mail answering, or even leaving the computer entirely to do something else. Many classroom activities go on for thirty, sixty, even ninety minutes. These simply will not work in a synchronous environment and will need to be revised or rejected as possible rapid development shortcuts.

The same is true when repurposing media from a classroom to a synchronous delivery as a rapid development shortcut. You need to be very careful of time and complexity. Video pieces should seldom last more than a minute, and slides need to be as basic as possible, both so that they can be easily seen on a computer screen and to reduce time to load.

On a more simplistic level, you can "borrow" the concept for a synchronous activity from other synchronous courses. For example, if you saw a good game in a synchronous class you attended, you might borrow the concept of how it worked, even if the content and structure don't match what you need.

If you have a top-rate synchronous software provider, they probably have demo programs with plenty of examples of activities. These might not reflect your content specifically, but the idea might be usable.

For example, your vendor (or someone) is displaying a synchronous activity where learners develop a simulated distribution process on a computerized map of the United States. As each participant adds to the network, his or her piece is shared by all the class, and discussions concerning the new addition are held in a talk box visible on everyone's screen until the new addition is accepted or rejected by vote. While your content might have to do with marketing, not distribution, you can use the concept of visual additions to your marketing plan that are discussed and then voted on to create a nationwide simulated marketing strategy.

RAPID DEVELOPMENT TECHNIQUES FOR ORIGINAL SYNCHRONOUS DEVELOPMENT

If you need to develop your materials for a synchronous e-learning delivery from scratch, there are still plenty of other rapid development techniques that you can use. The simplest of these we have already alluded to: Borrow ideas and even interactions from others. Most suppliers of synchronous software have a number of synchronous programs that they use as examples when selling their products. You probably saw some in their marketing materials. These programs are full of good ideas that you can add to your program to increase interactivity or to save you from doing a full development for aspects such as introductions, summaries, or even quizzes.

You can decrease your original synchronous material development time by knowing your facilitators as well. If you are the only facilitator, or if you know the capabilities of the facilitator cadre, you can slim down the facilitator guide to match. We discussed this technique earlier when talking about classroom rapid development techniques, so I won't repeat myself, but it is just as effective a rapid development technique in synchronous program development as it is in stand-up classroom development.

In actuality, almost every rapid development technique we discussed in the chapter on classrooms can be used to a lesser or greater extent in developing synchronous e-learning. The two deliveries are similar, although not quite as similar as some developers (and vendors) would like to believe.

You may have guessed this correlation from the fact that the end-products are similar: a participant package, an instructor's guide, and proper media. Just remember that while the end-products are related, there are marked differences as well.

Another cost-saving technique in original synchronous material development, though not necessarily a rapid development technique, is to make your participant packages totally electronic. This saves print costs and it works well in a synchronous environment, as the learners can simply toggle between the synchronous program itself and the participant package. When you revise your program, this will become a rapid development, or re-development, technique, as you will not need to redo, reprint, and redistribute the entire participant package.

A couple of hints for you here: (1) be sure that the learners are aware that the participant package exists as electronic copy so they bring it up before the lesson starts and possibly review it to help organize their learning and (2) let them know about it far enough in advance so that any old hats like me who still prefer the hard copy participant package can print one off. Actually, this can be a bit of a rapid implementation technique because you won't need to print and distribute hard copy participant packages. Definitely a time saver for someone, even if it isn't the developer.

Experts As a Synchronous Rapid Development Technique

One of the most effective rapid development techniques for synchronous e-learning development is to use experts as part of the instruction. This can be done in a number of ways, the simplest being to have the expert available on a separate phone to answer learner questions off-line. If a question is particularly relevant, the expert can signal to the instructor that there is an important concept to be discussed. Having an expert in this role means spending less time developing materials to the level at which they answer all likely questions, particularly if your facilitators are not subject-matter experts.

A second way to use an expert as a rapid development technique in a synchronous delivery is to have the expert give part of the presentation. Once again, this saves you development time, but you do need to make sure that the expert stays within the boundaries of the objectives, both by discussing them with the expert ahead of time and then by monitoring the instruction. Since this is synchronous e-learning, your experts do not need to be in the same room as the synchronous facilitator, or even in the same country as far as that goes. The facilitator controls the instructor interface, so the expert doesn't need to be familiar with the software other than knowing to press the "talk" and "next slide" buttons.

This technique is a real win-win-win situation, as the expert can instruct without worrying about the mechanics of the synchronous software, the facilitator gets a break, and the developer is required to develop less, as the expert doesn't need too detailed a facilitator guide—or sometimes none at all.

You will need to create an activity or two to go with your experts' talks for the facilitator to facilitate, and the facilitator will probably have a problem keeping the experts to your "suggested" time limit, but using experts in this way in a synchronous delivery definitely saves you development time and can be a refreshing, interesting change of pace for your learners.

Another way to use experts effectively and decrease development time is to have two of them do a discussion cum debate on a particular concept or issue. Once again, material development for this type of activity is minimal and a discussion board follow-up on the issue can be an excellent summary activity that costs almost no development time at all.

Still another technique is a virtual panel discussion, with a group of experts chatting about an issue or a general concept and its ramifications. These can be structured or freeform, with or without learner questions, and focused on an objective or used as a summary/introductory activity. Because it's synchronous and you can bring all the experts together virtually, your pool of possible candidates becomes as large as your organization. Development here consists of reminding the facilitators to do a debriefing after the discussion based on what they heard the panel members say.

No matter how you structure the use of your experts, you'll save development time over just about any other lesson format and give your learners the benefit of other informed and often fresh ideas on the topic.

Synchronous Instructors and Rapid Development

Your train-the-trainer processes for a synchronous delivery can use many of the same shortcuts we discussed in the classroom chapter, although the most effective one belongs to synchronous alone. To use it, you simply train your new trainers by having them log into the course as it is being given live. This is simple and cost-effective, as they can do it from wherever they are. Later they can even teach part of the program in a team-teach delivery before facilitating on their own. A train-the-trainer technique like this is usually cost-prohibitive in a face-to-face classroom delivery where trainers in training must be brought to the training site, but in synchronous deliveries it is not only cost-efficient, but incredibly effective.

One other rapid development technique for synchronous web-based deliveries that involves instructors is to have your seasoned synchronous instructors help you with the development. If they've been facilitating synchronous learning for a while, they'll have plenty of favorite interactions and little tricks that you might be able to use if you can capture them. You can do this as part of a review stage, which is the usual way, or even as a team development process starting at the very beginning of your development.

A word of caution: Be sure your colleagues truly are seasoned synchronous facilitators. This means that they've done more than one or two synchronous programs and know the in's and out's, and particularly the pitfalls, of synchronous facilitation. Otherwise some of the ideas and applications you harvest from them might not actually work, causing you more re-work. Hardly a rapid development shortcut!

OTHER SYNCHRONOUS (AND ASYNCHRONOUS) FACILITATION IN SYNCHRONOUS SOFTWARE AS RAPID DEVELOPMENT TECHNIQUES

You can make use of some of the other facilities available in your synchronous software as a rapid development techniques by implementing parts of a synchronous class though discussion boards and chat rooms. These work particularly well as pre- and post-class activities, or in multi-session, synchronous deliveries. This is another one of those "have the learners lead the learning" processes that decreases the amount of time you need to spend developing materials, as well as increasing learner responsibility for the learning.

For example, if you have a particularly thorny issue in your content that requires a strong discussion, instead of creating a series of PowerPoint slides and other discussion-leading materials in your synchronous program, simply have the facilitator post the issue to a discussion board (most good synchronous software packages have this functionality) and direct the learners to view it, research it, and post their thoughts for further discussion by all. You might have two or three or more of these discussion threads happening simultaneously, with significant learning occurring on all of them. And the only development required was the delineation of the issue.

A final summary posting by the facilitator of the results of the discussions, along with your own or an expert's thoughts on the issue, completes that piece of content with minimal development on your part. This technique works well in live chat rooms too, although they are somewhat harder to control and much more time-sensitive.

The ultimate use of these techniques is a combined synchronous/asynchronous and sometime face-to-face classroom delivery process probably more familiar to our academic colleagues, and often known to them as online learning, which just happens to be our next topic for discussion.

Chapter 6

Rapid Online Learning Development

Entry and Exit for Development

- Begin with strong learner-centered objectives based on a solid analysis
- End with a course plan and the materials required to implement it

End Products

- Course Syllabus
- Learner Activities
- Learner and Course Evaluations

One of the problems with our profession is that we can never agree on terminology. A mechanic's wrench is a wrench, a draftsmen's T square is a T square, but we trainers have more confusion around some of the basic concepts we employ than a Pacific sunset has colors. A good example of this is the concept of online learning. Sometimes this term means synchronous e-learning, sometimes it even means asynchronous e-learning, and sometimes it means something that really isn't either.

The reason I'm bothering to bring up this whole conundrum is that there is a variant of online learning that can be in itself a very effective rapid development technique, as well as having rapid development techniques of its own if you are using it as your main delivery process. This is actually true about more than one online learning variant, but let's not confuse a confusing issue further. We'll stick to one of the most commonly used concepts for what is termed an online delivery.

To see online learning's usefulness as a rapid development technique we'll first need to describe it (or at least this variant of it we'll be discussing) in some detail.

What we are talking about here is both synchronous and asynchronous in nature, because its major delivery aspects are chat rooms and threaded discussions via electronic discussion boards. In the academic model, the delivery usually begins with a face-to-face class, after which there are no more scheduled class meetings except through computer mediation until possibly the last week of the school term. This first face-to-face class is an effective but not critical aspect of the process and can be replaced by a synchronous e-learning class, a web meeting, a chat room, or even a simple conference call.

After the first meeting, the class is facilitated through a series of assignments that are completed by the learners individually, in pairs, in groups, or in learning teams. Learning resource lists for each assignment are provided and learners are encouraged to post other resources that they come across during their completion of each assignment. The products of these assignments are posted to the bulletin board for commentary and discussion, or presented in a synchronous chat room that has been scheduled for that purpose.

ONLINE ADVANTAGES

One of the major drawbacks in using any form of e-learning is that the whole process is complex and costly if the organization does not already employ it, and possibly less than effective if it already does due to inadequate planning and implementation when the system was initiated. e-Learning is not an intervention that should be attempted without a strong consideration of the cost and effectiveness issues inherent in the delivery. Even synchronous e-learning, which is arguably simpler to design and implement than asynchronous e-learning, has both software costs and facilitator training requirements that complicate its use considerably, as we've already seen.

The cost and time savings inherent in an online delivery when compared to other forms of e-learning are often obvious, and sometimes not so. One of the most touted advantages is the savings in both travel time and costs. This is true of synchronous e-learning deliveries as well, but an online delivery has the further advantage of being an easier process for both facilitators and learners to use. The facilitators do not need extensive training in how to utilize the software, and most learners these days are quite comfortable with posting to bulletin boards or interacting in a chat room.

There is a tremendous and less obvious advantage over traditional asynchronous e-learning as well. Even though much of the work done by the learners is asynchronous, in online learning there is still a facilitator available to interact with the learner, making the self-directed aspects of the learning less daunting to learners who have lower levels of self-directedness. Other advantages of an online delivery include:

- Allows real-time access to SMEs with minimal loss of their productivity
- Provides continuous learning
- Provides multiple reinforcements for greater retention
- Time to learner comfort level is less than with asynchronous
- Facilitator learning curve is less than with synchronous
- Learner learning curve is minimal
- Cheaper software
- Provides strong interactive and/or collaborative learning
- Allows for as much or as little self-direction as you feel the learners can handle
- Allows for many learners learning at the same time, though in different groups
- Research indicates team-building skills are enhanced considerably by participating in collaborative online learning projects

ONLINE DISADVANTAGES

Of course, there are disadvantages to an online delivery as well, not the least of which is that it often takes more time to develop the materials than for a synchronous e-learning program. This is due to the nature of the assignments. They need to be well-thought-out, leaving plenty of room for individual exploration, yet focus on a result that can be posted or discussed in the chat room. Your objectives also need to be sharper than ever. They guide the learners to the focus of the assignments, and as always, to the required learnings.

On the other hand, online development time is much less than for asynchronous e-learning. The nature of the delivery, and the fact that a facilitator is available, make a perfect set of materials less critical. Yet the majority of the learning that takes place is asynchronous, with all of the advantages that are implied by the use of that delivery process.

Another disadvantage is that an online delivery can actually take up more facilitator time in the monitoring of bulletin boards, threaded discussions, and chat rooms. However, instead of spending time in large blocks such as a day or a week, online time is measured in hours here and there, often over many weeks. As a developer you need to consider carefully how much facilitator time your activities will demand and then develop them appropriately. Here is a look at some of the other disadvantages of an online delivery.

- The same as for any delivery process, it is not good for everything.
- The learners may not come back for session two.
- Learners can easily lose interest or begin to multi-task during chat discussions.
- It requires learner personal discipline and corporate learning discipline.

LEARNING NEEDS THAT CAN BE MET THROUGH ONLINE LEARNING

You may have already realized that this delivery system is most effective for learning interventions that stretch over a number of weeks, such as a college class, but it can also be effective when the training need includes a multi-day class, such as those we often do for leadership or management training. In fact, because you can stretch the learning out over a longer period of time using an online delivery, reinforcement is enhanced, and the complaints of learners that they can't afford to be out of the office for two, three, or more full days are negated.

With this major advantage in mind, here is a list of possible uses for an online delivery.

An Online Delivery Is Effective for

- Long-term development activities
- Blending with OJT for skills building, cross-training, or remedial training

- Recertification
- Orientation
- Multiple-day classes of any kind
- Management development
- Almost any soft skills
- Team building
- Learning new computer software
- Simple communications processes

DEVELOPING ONLINE LEARNING FOR ORGANIZATIONS

By merging good instructional design principles with online methodology, we can create a delivery process that takes advantages of the aforementioned strengths while reducing or eliminating most of the weaknesses. Such a delivery has these characteristics:

It is analysis-based, relying on a good analysis to determine the training needs, and a solid job/task analysis to isolate the right content to base the activities on.

- It is objective-centered, with plenty of good, well-written objectives that help the learners visualize and achieve the proper end-products of the learning.

- It is learner-centered. The learners know the objectives, goals, where they are going, and why they want to get there. Much of online learning is self-directed and contract-based, both learner-centered methodologies.

- It is activity-based. The entire program revolves around the activities and assignments that have been design into it.

- It is criterion-evaluation-based.

Online Activities

The lifeblood of the online approach is the learning activities that the learners engage in during the intervention. This is also the most difficult aspect of the development process, as these activities need to be planned well in advance and focused directly on the learning objectives. The activities themselves are not significantly different from those you might develop for a classroom or asynchronous intervention, but since the learners are expected to work them on their own, they need to be much more detailed and created with the learner in mind rather than the facilitator. Following is a partial list of useful online activities.

Possible Online Activities

- One-on-one
- Small group
- Individual read and post
- Learner-led discussion
- Group discussion and post posting
- Contact fellow learners and . . .
- Web search
- Lead a web search
- Asynchronous resources
- Group projects with posts
- Posted position papers for live discussion or threaded discussion
- Pre-tests
- Debates
- Critiquing of provided or researched information
- Brainstorming
- Individual problem solving
- Group problem solving
- Games
- Analytical activities
    - Create timelines, draw maps, draw flow charts, create spreadsheets
- Guest experts or panels
- Team competitions

Most activities are introduced asynchronously through the use of a print-based assignment sheet. These assignment sheets are scheduled to be begun and completed at various times during the intervention according to a timetable published at the beginning of the process. Many of them include posting to the discussion board or a deadline followed by a live chat room discussion. Others might end with a submission to the facilitator or even a one-to-one exercise. Here is a simple example of an online assignment sheet.

EXAMPLE OF A LEARNER GUIDE ACTIVITY/ASSIGNMENT SHEET

Cost/Benefit Analysis Activity 1

Objective: Recommend a cost/benefit analysis tool based on an analysis of three available methodologies

Learner Instructions: The completion date for this activity is March 17.

Based on the article found on page 11 of your Learner Guide and the March 1 chat room discussion on cost/benefit analysis, do a web search for CBA tools that could be useful in your area of the organization.

Choose three of these tools and perform a comparative analysis of their strengths and weaknesses, then recommend the most effective tool for adoption by your group.

Complete a two-page report on your analysis and e-mail it to each member of the class by March 5.

Post a half-page or less synopsis of your report, along with the tool's URL on the bulletin board by March 5.

During the week of March 6 to 10, view the postings and respond, particularly if another member chose the same tool as you did.

The March 13 chat room will be a discussion of the advantages and disadvantages of the recommended tools, leading to a group decision on two tools that we will utilize to do a CBA during the week of March 20.

Further resources on CBA can be found under the CBA sub-heading in your "Suggested Learning Resources" file.

As a follow-on activity, share your thoughts with your manager and post a synopsis of your discussion. No responses to these postings please.

Extra credit to the first member who finds and posts the name of the person touted to be the father of CBA. If more than one father (mother?) is posted, state your reasoning.

Here are some hints for designing effective online learning interventions.

General Online Design Thoughts

- Be sure to create a strong participant package with activities, pre-class communications, objectives, reading material, learning resources, and a glossary.

- Always begin assignments or activities by stating the objectives they will cover.

- Use readings and websites in lieu of creating new content as you normally do in an asynchronous e-learning design.

- Build in progress checks that are completed by the learners and sent to the facilitator during long individual activities.

- Build in plenty of reviews and summaries, especially at the start of each segment.

- Place objectives everywhere, and even allow learners to create their own objectives.

- Utilize learning contracts as much as possible.

- Utilize collaborative or group learning contracts, particularly in team environments or for team-building processes.

- Create a help board for posts to group or instructor, for both technical and content problems.

- Make sure your learning resource lists are as complete and rich as possible.

- Structure large resource lists by objective.

- Allow for learner evaluation of their own learning. In group learning scenarios provide group evaluation activities of the group's learning.

- Use negotiated, mastery-evaluation-based contracts where possible.

- Add more structure in the form of:
  - Comprehensive schedules
  - Deadlines
  - e-Mail progress checks

- Create open-ended questions as part of your activities to elicit more thoughtful responses.

- Be sure your audience analysis is accurate and complete.

- Create a strong facilitator guide, even if you are the facilitator, with room for completion dates, notes, and other records.

- Create an FAQ posting.

- Develop evaluation instruments for both course and learners.

To wrap up this slightly long discussion, here is a job aid you can use when trying to decide whether online learning will make a good rapid development shortcut for your training need.

ONLINE DECISION JOB AID

The more "yeses" you circle, the more likely online will work for your learning intervention.

☐ Yes ☐ No Is the content mostly knowledge-based?

☐ Yes ☐ No Can any skill-based content be handled in the online environment or by blending?

☐ Yes ☐ No Can effective activities and exercises be developed?

☐ Yes ☐ No Are applicable paper-based graphics available, or can they be developed?

☐ Yes ☐ No Is the need for human interaction during the learning important to its success?

☐ Yes ☐ No Is there a need for collaborative learning?

☐ Yes ☐ No Are team-based problem-solving and decision-making activities and practice important?

☐ Yes ☐ No Is the background knowledge of the learners known?

☐ Yes ☐ No Is corporate learning discipline strong enough to expect the learners to attend scheduled chat rooms and make posting deadlines?

☐ Yes ☐ No Are critical content SMEs available often enough to share their expertise during chat room functions or on the discussion boards?

☐ Yes ☐ No Are the employees who need the content in different locations?

☐ Yes ☐ No Are competent developers available to create the online material?

☐ Yes ☐ No Must the content be taught on a periodic basis no matter what the size of the audience?

☐ Yes ☐ No Is the technology available for online learning?

☐ Yes ☐ No Are trained online facilitators available?

☐ Yes ☐ No Can the content be taught in an environment that is not face-to-face?

☐ Yes ☐ No Is there a relatively short development window?

☐ Yes ☐ No Is the content unstable?

ONLINE AS A RAPID DEVELOPMENT TECHNIQUE

I hope you can already see some of the rapid development shortcuts that can be taken advantage of here. You will need a minimal instructor guide made up of a few pages of directions and notes at the most, plus pages for keeping notes on the participants and class schedules or activities. The participant package is reduced to objectives, directions, a syllabus, some activity pages, and perhaps a page or two of learner information for the first class, if you have one. Most everything else in the participant package is references that you pull from other sources, and much of this is electronic in nature.

There is much less need for media, as the learners often provide their own media as part of the activities and discussion. Few if any complex graphics, no programming, and even the instructor training is reduced, as the software is much simpler. There are plenty of interactions and activities, particularly team interactions, all without the need for developing formal simulations or role plays.

Yet online is a fully functional delivery system. It provides all of the learning functionality of any other delivery method, and more than most. It can be used to teach basic skills, technical skills, management skills, soft skills, or team processes, even on-the-job training when combined with site facilitators (SMEs). As such, it is a useful rapid development technique when used in lieu of some of the other delivery systems or when combined with them in a blended delivery, which we will discuss in the next chapter.

Online can also be a significant rapid development technique when your content is unstable, or when you only need to teach it once. Because material development is so minimal in online, rapidly changing content can be handled easily, usually with a simple change or two in an activity or objective. One-and-done training for processes such as small software applications can be handled just as efficiently, as you do not need to spend hours developing materials and training aids for a single iteration of a class.

ONLINE RAPID DEVELOPMENT TECHNIQUES

There are a few development shortcuts for this development shortcut as well, although because it is already a relatively minimalist delivery system, not many. One that we previously mentioned is to hold the first class as a synchronous delivery. This can save you some time in material development, as we've already discussed, but a lot of travel time if you are in a dispersed organization, and travel time for your learners too.

Another online rapid development technique is to allow the learners to construct the course objectives. This works most effectively in development situations and, even then, mostly with those who come to the program with strong background knowledge, but it makes for a process that is more focused on the participants' learning needs. A word of caution: Always have some backup objectives to offer in case they miss something important.

Perhaps the most useful, and some would say daring, rapid development technique for online is the learning contract. We'll discuss these in more detail in an ensuing chapter, but by having your online learners develop singular or group learning contracts with objectives, resource plans, and evaluation mechanisms, you create a delivery whereby there is practically no development except that done by the learners, and the focus is purely on their needs.

This isn't the place to go into detail concerning how these processes work in an organizational learning environment, nor are they discussed in any detail in *Rapid Instructional Design*, to which I have been referring you for most of our design detail. However, if you are looking for more information on learning contracts, I suggest that you refer to the Proceedings of the annual International Symposium on Self-Directed Learning, which you can find at SDLGlobal.com.

Chapter 7

Blended Learning As a Rapid Development Technique

Entry and Exit for Development
- Begin with whatever entry items are required for *all* parts of the blend
- End with the pilot and pilot revisions for the blended intervention

End Products
- These are dependent on whatever end-products are produced by *all* aspects of the blend

---

A relatively new (if you consider a hundred and fifty years or so new) delivery system is blended learning. Of course, I'm being a bit tongue-in-cheek here, as blended learning has only come into its own in the last ten to fifteen years with the advent of computer-based and now web-based training that allows for the blending of asynchronous deliveries with classroom programs. However, blended learning actually does go back to the days of video and slide/tape presentations, and even further back to the blending of classroom with on-the-job training in manufacturing environments.

As with online learning, it is difficult to discuss blended learning as a singularity due to the wide variety of blends that can be utilized.

For rapid course development though, there are some major rapid development techniques available for developing a blended delivery.

The most basic (and useful) of these is the actual blending process itself. There are many possibilities for blending two or more delivery systems to reduce development time. A perfect example of this is the aforementioned blending of classroom with OJT. This blending not only provides necessary on-the-job practice, but means that your materials for the on-the-job training aspect need not be quite as formal as they would be for a straight classroom presentation.

It also allows you to develop the required practices without going through the involved process of creating full-fledged simulations. On-the-job training materials for performance practice and the evaluation of performance are much less intricate and therefore require less development time than their classroom equivalents would.

Another often-used blend combines an asynchronous program with a classroom program, usually with the asynchronous portion being developed as pre-work. This is actually not much of a rapid development technique for a classroom-based delivery. As we've seen, asynchronous programs take much longer to develop. It is mostly a cost-savings process whereby the learners do not need to be in the classroom quite as long.

However, this blend can be a rapid development technique if you are developing a program that is an asynchronous delivery to begin with, but you can make part of it classroom without losing too many of the advantages of the asynchronous delivery that caused you to choose it in the first place. This is particularly efficient if you can move the interactions and simulations into the live class, as they take so much longer to develop in an asynchronous mode.

For example, I had a client who was using a pretty good web-based supervisory skills program, but it wasn't achieving its objectives, as there were no interactions developed for it that really helped to solidify the learning. We redesigned the program to a blended delivery that was comprised of twenty hours of asynchronous learning and a two-day classroom session, which we spent in activities and simulations. Had we developed simulations to match the classroom ones in an asynchronous mode, it would have taken literally months of development time, and the client had no real reason for using the asynchronous delivery other than the notion that it seemed like a good idea at the time.

Now you might say, "If I can use a classroom, why the heck am I developing asynchronous to begin with?" And if you did, go to the head of the class! Asynchronous deliveries are most efficient in situations in which a classroom isn't, or if a classroom is simply impossible due to distance or timing problems. But before you pat yourself on the back, don't forget that a classroom does not always mean a face-to-face classroom.

An often overlooked yet very effective blended development shortcut is the telephone. A simple conference call between the facilitator and the participants of almost any program can take the place of long hours of material development. I have seen phone calls used in lieu of pieces of asynchronous content, as a simple way to train on a performance aid once it is in the hands of all the users across the country and as the medium for adding easy to develop role plays and other interactive activities to an asynchronous program.

I was part of a program for which we designed an entire management development curriculum around what we termed "brown bag" phone calls. These were lunch time conference calls between participants in the company's management development program and top executives of the organization. Each executive gave a ten-to-fifteen-minute prepared talk on a management issue he or she felt was important to the company within his or her particular area of expertise, and then answered questions (a couple of which we always prepared just in case). The topic was announced by a one-page information paper that gave the background of the topic and the objectives of the talk, and a follow-up page with the questions and answers and sources of further information. Basically, we had an organizational-focused management development process taught by the people who knew the most about the content, with the only material development being a couple of one-page handouts created twice a month.

BLENDING SYNCHRONOUS AND ASYNCHRONOUS E-LEARNING AS A RAPID DEVELOPMENT TECHNIQUE

Blending an asynchronous program with a synchronous classroom can be wonderfully effective, and it can save you a lot of asynchronous development time as well, not to mention giving you better interactions. In my example above, we added both interaction and structure to the program through the blending of asynchronous e-learning with a classroom, and still saved half of the time and travel costs, as well as a large chunk of development time. However, if we'd had the ability to create a synchronous classroom, the time and cost savings would have been much greater.

This form of blending can also allow you to take advantage of another rapid development technique, the repurposing of classroom-based group activities. It is difficult, to say the least, to create a group activity in an asynchronous environment. It can be done, but it is very cumbersome and time-consuming. With a synchronous/asynchronous blend though, many of your classroom activities can be repurposed into the synchronous portion of the program, saving you much of the development time that you would have spent trying to make them into asynchronous activities.

There are many other blends; asynchronous with OJT, face-to-face classroom with synchronous (which is basically the online learning process we talked about earlier), even on-the-job training and mentoring, which is a delivery called structured mentoring that we will discuss next. The important thing to remember is that blends can be very useful rapid development techniques if you pick your blend wisely.

Most blends are chosen based on necessity (you have too many people in too many places and not enough trainers) or for the cost savings (combining synchronous and asynchronous deliveries so that learners do not need to travel at all) rather than for rapid development, but if development time is a big concern, and it should be, consider blends to reduce it.

If you are thinking of blending synchronous and asynchronous e-learning for a more rapid development process, here are some questions you might want to ask:

- Do the e-learners have intranet/Internet access?
- Do the learners have soundcards in their computers?
- Do they have headsets, microphones, speakers?
- Is the organizations slowest connection speed fast enough?
- Do the computers have CD or DVD players; if so, which?
- Is there access to other functionalities such as chatrooms and instant messaging?
- Is there required software available or downloadable on all learner computers?
- Do you have a compatible learning management system?

- Do you have or can you buy expertise in asynchronous and synchronous development?
- Do you have or can you buy expertise in asynchronous and synchronous implementation?
- Are SMEs with content expertise available on a continuing basis?
- Is technical support available for hardware and software problems?
- Is there time available for development?

Chapter 8

Rapid Structured Mentoring Development

Entry and Exit for Development
- Begin with solid objectives that were created through a strong job/task analysis and validated by both subject-matter experts and higher-level management
- End with a live, observed pilot of a mentor using the materials with a learner

End Products
- Mentor Guide
- Learner's Guide
- Evaluations of All Objectives and the Course
- Reference Material

$\mathbf{W}$e mentioned earlier that one form of blended learning was a combination of on-the-job training and mentoring, often termed "structured mentoring." Structured mentoring is also a great rapid development technique. This management training process takes advantage of the fact that you have seasoned managers in your organization who have plenty of experience to share with new managers, but either don't know how to go about it, or simply don't think to do it.

USING STRUCTURED MENTORING FOR RAPID DEVELOPMENT

The way it works is simple. Assuming your analysis is complete, you create the objectives for your structured mentoring program; jot down some ideas on how to teach and learn them; add whatever corporate documentation is important for the training or as reference material; develop some quizzes, performance checklists, final evaluations, and a tracking mechanism; then go over the whole process with the mentors you have chosen based on their content expertise and their willingness to be mentors; and let them take it from there.

Of course, the details are a bit more complicated than that, but our purpose here isn't to explain the design, but rather to look at it from a rapid development point of view.

I hope that by now you can see the development advantages for yourself. Your instructor guide (mentor guide) can be very reduced, as you are using the expertise of the mentors to fill in most of it. Your participant package (learner's guide) becomes basically a restatement of the objectives with room for notes, plus whatever documentation you can add or instructions on how to obtain the documentation while on the job. Media is minimal to non-existent, and evaluation can be mostly checklists and self-quizzes based on the objectives and monitored by the mentor. Compared to a classroom delivery, or even good OJT, this is a much less intensive materials development process.

You can also use structured mentoring as the foundation for a number of different blends in order to decrease development time and increase learning effectiveness. One of my favorites is to blend in off-the-shelf videos or asynchronous management skills programs that the learner completes and then discusses with the mentor. A single page of discussion points for both the mentor and the trainee in their respective guides provides enough information to complete the learning task, and that's all the materials development you need to do as the rest is taken care of by your purchased material and your two-person learning team. And the ability to practice the management skills they've just discussed in the work environment right after their discussion is priceless.

STRUCTURED MENTORING RAPID DEVELOPMENT TECHNIQUES

Like some of the other delivery processes that are also rapid development techniques on their own, structured mentoring does not have many rapid development shortcuts for its own development. The main reason for this is that, from a development point of view, it is about as simple as it gets.

The only rapid development techniques I've found are the blending processes such as the use of videos or vendor-developed asynchronous programs that we've already discussed. For the most part, structured mentoring is a foundational delivery system that is its own rapid development technique, and it can be used for other deliveries as well in a blended process.

A good example of this is a program I created for a financial institution to train their branch managers. The foundation of the system was the designation of mentoring branches where a very strong and experienced branch manager was the mentor. During the weeks the trainees spent at the mentoring branches, there were periodic classroom programs held to allow for a group dynamic and team-building exercises, and even a couple of synchronous classes during which they heard from top management on various critical issues for the organization. The classes and even the synchronous programs required the majority of our development time. The structured mentoring piece, which provided the majority of the training experience, required almost no development time at all.

STRUCTURED MENTORING FOR RAPID NON-MANAGEMENT TRAINING DEVELOPMENT

We've been discussing a structured mentoring delivery as it relates to management training and development, but it can also be used for non-management training as well, particularly in an office environment. This isn't usually as effective as using it for management training, as it is more difficult to find individual contributors with the expertise and the time to act as mentors. Structured mentoring isn't on-the-job training, where the subject-matter expert does a training piece and is done; it requires a fairly heavy time commitment on the part of the mentor. However, if your situation warrants this type of training, it can be an useful rapid development technique for non-management employees as well.

I used it effectively at a health care insurance company for training new customer service representatives and call center employees. There were five different positions at various grade levels, and each position had half a dozen or more incumbents, at least one or two of whom were acknowledged experts. Because of the complexity of the situation and the task overlaps, the analysis was long and involved; but once the objectives were clarified, we were able to complete the mentor and learner's guides very quickly, as almost all of the information was in procedure manuals and/or the heads of the mentors. The mentors were able to stay on the job while training their new colleagues in what was actually almost an apprenticeship situation, but with the structure of the guides to make sure nothing was missed and that every task was evaluated.

Figures 8.1 and 8.2 are examples from a Mentor's Guide and a Participant's Guide, respectively, for a structured mentoring program I created in a non-management environment.

ABM MENTORING PROGRAM OBJECTIVES

TASK 6: SUCCESSFULLY MAINTAIN ONGOING PROGRAMS

Directions	To help the trainees master this objective, first review any **references or other materials** indicated in the Learner's Guide for this task. Next use the list of **discussion points** to guide your discussion with the trainees concerning the objective. Then demonstrate to the trainees how to perform any processes related to this objective. Allow the trainees time to practice the performances. When the learners are ready, use the Final Performance Checklist to evaluate mastery.
Discussion Points/ Performances	• How to perform store checks • Reviews of new item status • Reviews of plan-o-grams • How to perform an effective competitive market review • Discuss the purpose of reviewing weekly ads • Demonstrate effective methods for tracking trucks • The accurate completion of all forms related to maintaining programs such as call logs, weekly reports, and the principal issues and opportunities report

---

Figure 8.1. Mentor Guide Example

ABM MENTORING PROGRAM FORMS AND REPORTS LIST

Following is a list of forms and reports that you will use on the job. The forms in italics are corporate forms and can be found after the notes page for each objective. The non-italicized forms are customer- or site-specific. They will be provided by your trainer as appropriate.

Objective	Task	Name/Description of Form
1	1.1 to 1.3	Item Distribution Report
1	1.2	Promotional Availability Report
2, 3	2.15/3.3	Monthly Status Report
3	3.2	Distribution Voids
3	3.2	Short Report (Inventory Summary)
4	4.1	Internal Deductions Log
6	6.5	Ad Tracking Log
6	6.7	Weekly Reports
6	6.7	Call Logs
6	6.7	Principal Issues and Opportunities Report
12	12.1	New Supplier Alert Form (found in order processing procedures)
12	12.1	Supplier Master List (found in order processing procedures)
12	12.1	Order Revision Sheet (found in order processing procedures)
7	7.1	Supplier Verification Forms
4	4.1	Deductions Report (sent to general manager)
12	12.2&3	Cash Receipts Report

Figure 8.2. Participant Guide Example

Chapter 9

Self-Directed Learning and Rapid Development

Entry and Exit for Development

- Begin with validated objectives.
- Begin with a conceptualization of a developmental planning system.
- End with a full pilot of the self-directed material held in a controlled environment.
- End with training for both managers and employees on individualized prescriptive development.

End Products

- Self-Directed Learning Program with All Media and Evaluation Aspects Required
- Learning Contracts for Individualized Prescriptive Development

---

. . . . Self-directed learning (SDL) has never been a widely accepted term, or concept for that matter, in the world of training. For the most part it was always something our colleagues in academia were interested in, but not really relevant to organizational learning. At least that was true until e-learning came along. There are two major and somewhat different conceptualizations of SDL, and both of them have become key delivery systems for corporate training, although we seldom call either of them self-directed learning.

ASYNCHRONOUS SELF-DIRECTED LEARNING AS A RAPID DEVELOPMENT TECHNIQUE

The first of these is an old friend from a previous chapter, asynchronous learning. Even before there were computers or videotapes or even slide and audiotape programs that learners could complete at their own pace, there were print learning programs that performed the same function. The famous (some would say infamous) correspondence schools that educated tens of thousands in an earlier generation and were the precursors of the online universities of today, are a good example of print-based self-directed learning.

So why is this important to us in our exploration of rapid development techniques? Because, as an asynchronous learning process, print self-directed learning is simply faster and easier to develop than asynchronous e-learning. That's not to say that for the sake of efficiency we should go back a few decades and produce print self-directed learning programs in lieu of asynchronous e-learning, although for some designs that concept is not completely without merit.

What it does mean for the rapid course developer is that a good participant package (often termed a learning guide in this incarnation), developed to accompany our asynchronous e-learning program, can not only shorten the amount of time and effort we put into the development of that asynchronous e-learning program, but can speak to the trainees using a different learning modality as well.

For example, instead of going through all the effort of adding self-check quizzes to your e-learning, what if you simply placed them in the learning guide? I know, there are lots of good reasons for doing them electronically, but if you're on a deadline that is looking far too close, this is an alternative.

The same is true of graphics, spreadsheets, even entire readings. Instead of waiting for graphic artists to render, programmers to program, and the interminable testing that comes with all e-learning material, just slip them into your self-directed learning guide with some directions on how and where to use them on a screen in your e-learning program.

You can even develop entire programs using this method. A good many years ago, more than I wish to count and long before e-learning or even computer-based learning were available delivery systems, I was charged with developing a program to teach our nursing staff at a medical center I was working for how to operate the organization's new computerized admission and discharge system. I accomplished this by developing a self-directed manual that took my learners step-by-step through the various processes they were required to master, while they followed along on the computer screen, pushing keys on the computer keyboard when they were directed to do so by the program. I didn't even need to include screen shots in the print-based learning guide, as they saw the screens live on the monitor (CRT in those days) as they went through the program. I added exercises in the manual where they completed each task for themselves (screen shots were necessary here so that they could compare what they saw on their screen at the end of a process to what they should have seen), and a monitored final exam where they demonstrated to the monitor (human variety this time) that they could perform the tasks. I developed the entire program in less than a week and trained over 1,000 nursing staff in the next two weeks, on all three shifts. Today, using our more "modern" technology it would take me a week simply to lay out a storyboard!

If you are thinking, "OK, but we aren't in the stone age anymore, George," I recently used the exact same rapid development technique to re-train a mixed group of employees in a SAP implementation. The implementation had been failing, at least partly due to the fact that the primary training was being delivered through a web-based, static, PowerPoint delivery that was basically comprised of a few jillion screenshots the trainees clicked their way through. It might have been efficient to develop, but it certainly wasn't very effective.

They needed something good, and fast, as the implementation was well underway by the time I was called in, so I developed a print self-directed learning package that used their screen shots and instructor notes to train the employees both individually and in groups with a monitor where possible. There was no programming, no fancy graphics, just information, job aids, and a lot of print-directed but computer-based practice activities.

Now I love PowerPoint. In fact, when used properly it is a good rapid development technique, as we've already discussed, not to mention that it has saved me thousands of tedious hours of creating overhead projections. However, it has become so pervasive, and so many people think knowing how to use it makes them trainers and so they employ it for so much terrible training, that it's actually quite scary considering the cost to the organization of poor training.

Subject-matter experts and even otherwise good trainers spend too much time developing needless and sometimes worthless PowerPoint presentations in lieu of solid training material development, as was the case in my SAP training example. Take a look around your own organization, particularly at software applications training, and if you see the same thing, consider the rapid development technique of developing a print self-directed learning package to help augment the asynchronous training you already have.

Figure 9.1 is an example of a program on, of all things, instructional design in which I combined a vendor's software package with a print self-directed package to produce a program that taught new designers how to design.

MODULE 4: DESIGN

Objectives: The user will be able to . . .

- Create proper trainee-centered objectives based on task analysis information
- Create criterion-referenced test questions based on stated trainee objectives
- Select effective presentation methods based on defined criteria for training on various tasks and task groupings.
- Choose effective follow-up methods for courses where applicable

Time: 105 minutes

Open the sample project you have been working with.

Section 1: The Objectives Tab

Objectives: The user will be able to . . .
- Discuss the purpose of objectives
- Describe the four main parts of a proper objective
- Create effective objectives using the LID
- Modify the default conditions and standards in the LID

*Click on the **Design** area of the LID and then click on the tab marked **Objectives** if it is not already selected.*

Part 1: Creating Objectives
One of the most important aspects of any training program is the objectives. Objectives help to guide the instructional designer in the development of the course materials (and the trainees as

well) by telling them what they need to know or do to successfully master that material. Performance objectives describe what trainees will be able to do when they have completed the instruction. They are also the key aspect of any evaluation that the course provides, not only evaluation of the trainees, but of the course itself. If trainees can demonstrate mastery of the concepts that are described in the objectives, you can assume they have learned what you wanted them to learn.

Objectives can also give trainees an overall look at the relevance of the material, which often contributes to their motivation for learning.

An objective is a measurable statement of each behavior that the trainee will be able to demonstrate during the course, the conditions for the demonstration, and the criterion for acceptable performance. You've been developing the foundation for your objectives ever since you started the planning process. Objectives are based on the duties, tasks, sub-tasks, and steps that you produced throughout the planning and analysis stages. Often, particularly if you've used action verbs in the creation of these statements, they will become your objectives.

One important consideration here is not to mix course goals with trainee objectives. Many times designers write objectives about what the course will do and think they have gone far enough with objectives. These "course objectives" are important in your early decision making about what the course will contain and even the determination of whether you will attempt the course at all. They also come into play in some aspects of course evaluation.

However, at this point we are beyond the course description level in the instructional design process and are considering exactly what the trainees need to know and do in the course itself. "Trainee objectives" should speak directly to the trainees about these aspects so they can gauge their own learning. An easy way to remind yourself of this is to start each trainee objective you write with the statement: "At the end of this segment of learning the trainee will be able to. . . . Now fill in an action verb and what it is that the trainee will be able to do. For course, you can start your objective statement with: "This course is created to. . . ."

You may not want to actually put these statements at the front of each objective that you give to your trainees, although many designers do, but while you're developing them it doesn't hurt to

(Continued)

do so, just to remind you of who these objectives are for. Here are some examples of good objectives:

- The trainee through a virtual reality simulation will be able to troubleshoot equipment failures with 90 percent accuracy.
- The trainee, when provided a sample of the mixing product, will be able to identify the levels of negative substrate which exceed recommended limits with 100 percent accuracy.
- The trainee-operator, when receiving simulated data from the robot will be able to execute the primary commands to reduce the cutting edge to nominal limits every time the product becomes too wide.
- The trainee will be able to list every item necessary for the manufacturing of a truck tire.

Which brings up another aspect of objectives. Because they are for your trainees, make sure that you design into your course a mechanism for the trainees to find the objectives and use them. Giving them a list of objectives at the beginning of the course is a good idea. So is referring to the objectives you've just covered each time you do a summary. A final summary that includes the objectives helps and, of course, you will use them as the basis for any learning evaluation.

The LID software proposes three parts for the writing of objectives. They are Condition, Standard, and Objective, which is often termed "performance." A brief discussion of each can be found in the "Contents Help" section of the software under "Write Objectives."

The performance usually begins with an action verb. As discussed earlier, Bloom developed a method of categorizing action verbs into six major classes:

- Knowledge—recalling information
- Comprehension—explaining ideas
- Application—using ideas
- Analysis—seeing relationships
- Synthesis—combining ideas
- Evaluation—making judgments

In this list, the classes are in order from the least to the most difficult form of learning, with the mastery of simple knowledge being the easiest thing for most of your trainees, while combining of this knowledge into new ideas and evaluating those ideas are the hardest for them to do. Be sure that you choose verbs that fit the difficulty of learning that you expect when finalizing your objectives.

Following are a list of performance verbs classified into Bloom's categories:

Many designers ignore the "condition" aspect or pay it little mind. However, the condition can help you later when you choose your instructional strategies. Good objectives describe the environment in which the performance will take place, particularly if it can be related to where the skill will later be used. A true-to-life condition motivates the trainees and makes them more confident, thus maximizing learning transfer and retention.

Objectives Screen 16

Notice on the screen for the project you have accessed that the objective you are developing will be related to a task that you picked for training in the analysis area. If you created this task correctly, it will already have an action verb assigned to it. The objective is basically this task statement with the conditions and standards added. The screen provides these two parts of the objective, which have

PERFORMANCE VERBS BY BLOOM TAXONOMY							
Knowledge	Comprehension	Application	Analysis	Synthesis	Evaluation		
Count	Recall	Associate	Interpret	Apply	Order	Arrange	Appraise
Define	Recite	Compare	Interpolate	Calculate	Group	Combine	Assess
Draw	Read	Compute	Predict	Classify	Translate	Construct	Critique
Identify	Record	Contrast	Translate	Complete	Transform	Create	Determine
Indicate	Repeat	Describe		Demonstrate	Analyze	Design	Evaluate
List	State	Differentiate	Employ	Detect	Develop	Grade	
Name	Tabulate	Discuss	Examine	Explain	Formulate	Judge	
Point	Trace	Distinguish	Illustrate	Infer	Generalize	Measure	
Quote	Write	Estimate		Practice	Separate	Integrate	Rank
Recognize	Extrapolate	Relate		Summarize	Organize	Rate	
		Solve	Construct	Plan	Select		
		Use	Prepare	Test			
		Utilize	Prescribe	Recommend			
		Produce					
		Propose					
		Specify					

(Continued)

been determined in advance as defaults for all objectives. When you click the "Create Objective" button, the parts are added together and an objective is created.

There will be times when the objective just didn't come together quite right through this method, so you will have to modify it a bit. This can be done by clicking in the objective box and then making changes. If you want to change the conditions or standards for an objective, you can do this as well in the objective box.

You have now created a first-level objective, which can help guide you and the trainees in the training process. However, most often this level does not have enough detail to be really effective for your trainee. You can develop second-level objectives by using the steps for each task that you determined back in the analysis area. These steps would be listed at the bottom of the screen.

If you wrote them properly, each step should already be a performance with an action verb attached. To make them into objectives, you only need to add conditions and standards. If these will be the same as your first-level objective, you may choose not to restate them. However, look at each step carefully before making this decision.

Choose each step that you wish to make an objective for and add it to the objective block. You can do this by retyping the statement or by highlighting it and choosing "Select All," then "Copy," then "Paste" from the edit pull-down menu. If a change is needed to the conditions, standards, or anything else, you can make it now.

To make it easier to track your objectives later, number your first-level objectives with the same number as the task they are based on. Then number your second-level objectives with the appropriate step number.

You might also want to leave space between objectives you write in the objective box to make it easier to read them.

When you are finished, you will have a list of all first- and second-level objectives for this particular task.

One hint here. The LID software does not ask you to write objectives based on sub-tasks. In a complicated course with a lot of tasks, sub-tasks, and steps, writing sub-task-level objectives can sometimes help you in your objective development. You can obtain a list of sub-tasks by using the "Task Analysis" report. Once again, if you wrote these sub-tasks properly, they should already have action verbs and be close to looking like objectives. Making them into objectives can help you keep things straight as you write your second-level objectives.

You can number these objectives if you choose to create them with the appropriate sub-task number.

And a last thought: No matter how proficient you become at creating objectives, you can still make many errors in judgment. It's critical that you have an SME review your objectives before your trainees ever see them—just in case.

- Open the "simulation" project.

- Navigate to the **objectives** tab.

- If you've done everything right until now, you should have a screen that begins with "Task 1.3, implementing a change model."

- Click on the "Create Objectives" button.

- Notice that the objective has combined the default conditions and standards with your task.

- It's not very good English, which often happens, so change "implementing" to **"implement"** by clicking in the objective box and making the change.

- Number your objective 1.3, as your task is numbered.

- Now add a second-level objective by bringing the first of the steps up to the objective box. You can do this by following either of the methods discussed earlier.

- Number this objective 1.3.1.1 so that it matches Step 1.3.1.1 that it was written for.

- We'll keep the same conditions and standards so we won't rewrite them.

- Now add another second-level objective by bringing the step **"Schedule completion dates"** into the objective box. This objective needs more explanation, so change its condition to **"Given specific deliverables the trainee will be able to"** and the change the standard to **"that are within the limits provided for by the change plan."** Number this objective 1.3.1.2.

After entering the appropriate data, keep your simulation open and go on with Part 2.

(Continued)

Part 2: Modifying Default Conditions and Standards

When you developed your first-level objective for the simulation, you used the default conditions and standards. You changed both of these for one of the second-level objectives by making the change in the objective block. However, if you have a series of first- and second-level objectives that all need standards and/or conditions different from the defaults, or if your entire course needs the defaults to be changed, you can do this in the appendix area of the LID.

If you want to change the default conditions and standards for all of your objectives, this must be done before you develop the first objective. Otherwise you will have to change these aspects separately for each objective.

- Open the "simulation" project if it is not already open.

- Navigate to the **objectives** tab.

- Note the default conditions and standards.

- Now click on the **appendix** tab.

- Change the defaults as follows:

  - Click on the button labeled "user." This will allow you to enter into the conditions and standards box

  - For conditions: **Given the parameters for a department-wide change initiative.**

  - For standards: **All aspects must be completed in accordance with the six-step Implementing Change Model.**

- Navigate back to the **objectives** section.

- Note the default conditions did not change because you've already written objectives. However, if you follow this process before you start writing you will see the default change. Pick what works best for you.

When you have finished entering the appropriate data, complete the **"Check Your Knowledge"** section which follows. Then open the example project you have been working with, and go on with Section 2.

Check Your Knowledge

Answer each question to the best of your ability without looking back at the material. Then check your answers against the correct one provided on the next page. Look back through the section to find the proper information for any question you missed.

1. Objectives are used by

   A. Designers
   B. Trainees
   C. Evaluators
   D. All of the above

2. True or False: Objectives are written at two levels of detail

3. Which of the following is a part of a good objective?

   A. Standard
   B. Trainee statement of fact
   C. Course goal
   D. All of the above

4. True or False: Objectives can be written based on tasks, subtasks, or steps?

5. True or False: You should strive to write at least five objectives for program?

Answers

1. D

2. T

3. A

4. T

5. F

Figure 9.1. Self-Directed Instructional Design Program

PRINT SELF-DIRECTED LEARNING AS A SKILLS TRAINING RAPID DEVELOPMENT TECHNIQUE

There are some deliveries for which this rapid development technique isn't particularly effective though. The major one that comes to mind is in mobile learning, or m-learning. We will be discussing rapid development techniques for this relatively new delivery process in a later chapter, but since its major advantage is that it is mobile, lugging around a print package to go with it sort of defeats the purpose.

The development of a self-directed learning print program for use with a computer software application such as the SAP example is actually another kind of blend, but you can also use a self-directed learning print program on its own as a rapid development technique for skills training. I have to admit I haven't done this lately, as web-based asynchronous training is pretty much the standard, but I've used it most effectively in the past in both retail and office environments.

If I ran into a situation even today where I had a large, highly dispersed training audience and very little time to do the development for a critical program, particularly if that audience was computer illiterate or had no computer access, I wouldn't hesitate to use a print self-directed learning design as a rapid development technique to make sure I got the training to my learners when they needed it and in a way that they could use it.

PROBLEM-BASED LEARNING AS A RAPID DEVELOPMENT TECHNIQUE

Problem-based, or some organizations call it case-based learning, is sort of an offshoot of self-directed learning. It is also an excellent rapid development technique. In problem-based learning, problems or cases are presented to a class and teams are formed to determine the necessary steps for solving the problem or diagnosing the case. The teams divide up the problem and each member works on his or her own aspect of the possible solution. Next the team regroups and shares the information they have collected, then develops a common solution or diagnosis of the case and presents it along with their methodology for reaching their conclusions when the entire class meets again. Discussion concerning each team's solution and other possible alternatives based on a synthesis from presented solutions follows.

The savings in development time here is pretty obvious. Instead of the developer creating learning materials and resources, the teams and the individuals who comprise them find their own, on their own. Your participant package isn't much more than the problem or case and perhaps some directions that can lead them toward resources, while your instructor guide is once again the problem, along with possible solutions and discussion points. Media, except for a few summary slides that might even be done on the fly, depending on the information the teams present, comes from the teams as part of their presentations.

Just a note in case you missed it. Online learning is a wonderful delivery system for this type of learning methodology.

SELF-DIRECTED LEARNING AS A RAPID DEVELOPMENT TECHNIQUE

Self-directed learning has a second major aspect that we in the training world pay slight notice to, at least on a theoretical basis, but it is a major topic of discussion in academia, and that is SDL as truly "self-directed" learning, that is, the decision on what to learn being based on the learners' own perceptions of their learning needs. Now if you're thinking that's fine in academia, but doesn't fly in the "real world," I submit to you a concept that is gaining more and more credibility every day in corporations around the globe: prescriptive employee self-development.

If this term is new to you, the concept itself probably isn't. It started in the management development field and had as its basis the realization that managers when taken as a group have a variety of development needs. Some have high competency in operations but are not so good with people. Others are great coaches but not so hot on team building. Some have high leadership potential but never quite make the jump to becoming quality leaders. You get the picture.

The good old management development programs of the past, with series after series of classes and an actual management development curriculum that is completed over three or five or one hundred and five years, didn't deal well with this issue of individuality, and was therefore somewhat less than successful at turning supervisors or individual contributors into managers. Even three months at Harvard Business School for an "intensive" program or retreats where managers crossed bridges blindfolded to learn trust didn't quite do it.

What we are beginning to understand (although we've actually known it all along, I think), is that all managers come into the management development process with their own strengths and weaknesses, their personal hard-won areas of expertise, and their own individual competencies, not quite competencies, and "what the heck are they talking abouts?" Therefore, each manager should have an individualized prescription for what he or she needs to learn, and what skills and competencies to develop to move on to the next level, or simply to get better at his or her current job.

These prescriptions often come in the form of learning contracts that the managers negotiate with their managers, coaches, or mentors and that allow the managers to choose how they are going to learn the things they have decided they need to learn. The learning contracts usually include objectives, learning plans/activities, time frames, and an evaluation mechanism to keep the process systematic.

I expect that you can see how this is self-directed learning: the managers choosing how to learn, and sometimes even what to learn, through the development of their own learning objectives, and I hope you can see how this is a rapid development technique.

No? Well, consider how quickly you can institute a management development program when you don't need to develop a curriculum, or even classes, when your management trainees go out on their own (with some guidance from their managers and maybe from you) and determine what they decide are the best ways for them to have the training they need delivered to them, seminars, college classes, Harvard, ropes and bridges, whatever works for them.

If some of your management trainees want to hear about how to achieve continuous improvement from Jack Welch, there is a public program or a video available that will tell them, while if others don't even know or care about who Jack Welch was, they don't need to sit through a discussion of six sigma, but can find another way to learn about continuous improvement. Can you see the development savings now? Good!

Prescriptive development isn't just for managers. Many companies are developing their supervisors and even individual contributors through developmental learning contracts and prescriptive processes that allow for a wide range of self-direction in choosing delivery, and in some cases content. I've seen some really cutting-edge companies that are even requiring such contracts as the basis for their tuition-reimbursement structure.

A basic tool for this type of self-directed development is the asynchronous course libraries that can be purchased for access from an organization's learning management system. These program repositories allow individuals to choose from hundreds of topics, an open university of possibilities for their development within the corporation or for simple self-development. And you, the training developer, did not have to develop a single piece of material in order for all of this training to be available to your learners. What a rapid development technique!

In the final analysis, self-direction of this type, creating learning contracts, developing your own personal learning objectives, choosing individual programs and learning activities that fit your needs, and creating self-evaluation mechanisms is basically a process of plugging into our learners' "need to learn," which, as research has shown time and again, is critical to any motivation for learning and a foundational aspect of what we do as trainers.

You can also use self-directed learning as the training component for job aids and performance tools, which it just happens is our next topic. Before we go there though, here are some steps to follow for both the learner and the organization when implementing a self-directed development process (see the list below) and a couple of examples of self-directed development contracts (Figures 9.2 and 9.3).

Steps in Implementing a Self-Directed Development Process

For the Organization
- Sell approach to management
- Perform an assessment of participant readiness
- Announce the program
- Publish statements of support from top management
- Develop contract template
- Identify participant support systems
- Orient participants
- Orient managers
- Solicit feedback on program
- Perform program evaluation
- Perform ROI

For Individual Participants
- Analyze own learning style
- Determine own learning preferences
- Attend orientation
- Determine learning needs
- Prioritize learning needs
- Develop learning objectives
- Isolate learning resources
- Select learning activities
- Set timing and milestones
- Develop evaluation criteria
- Create contract
- Obtain signoffs
- Schedule learning activities
- Seek feedback where needed
- Document learning
- Renegotiate contract if required
- Compare learning outcomes to evaluation criteria
- Begin new contract

SELF-DIRECTED DEVELOPMENT CONTRACT

Learner: _____

Manager: _____

Topic: _____

Date begun _____

Date Completed _____

Organizational Goal This Learning Will Help to Achieve	Personal Goal This Learning Will Help to Achieve	Learning Objectives (What Will Learner Know or Be Able to Do?)	Learning Process (What Steps Will the Learner Take?)	Learning Resources (What Will We Provide?)	Target Dates	Evaluation (The Learner Will Have Succeeded When . . . (Job Application)

_____
Manager's Signature

_____
Learner's Signature

Figure 9.2. Learning Contract 1

SELF-DIRECTED DEVELOPMENT CONTRACT

Learner: _____   Date begun: _____

Manager: _____   Date completed: _____

What will be learned through this contract?

How will this help to achieve corporate/departmental/personal goals?

What are the objectives of the learning?

How will the learning take place?

What resources will it be necessary for the learner to obtain?

What resources will the manager need to provide?

What are the milestones to be achieved to keep the project on track?

What evidence will the learner provide that the objectives have been met (application to the job)?

How will the manager determine that the contract has been completed?

❏ Objective achieved Progress toward achievement
                         ❏ Adequate
                         ❏ Inadequate

_____   _____
Learner's Signature   Manager's Signature

Figure 9.3. Learning Contract 2

Chapter 10

Performance Aids As Rapid Development Techniques

Steps in the Process
- Begin with any task for which you have analyzed the required skills and knowledge
- End with a live pilot where an on-the-job training instructor teaches a trainee how to use your performance aid, and then the trainee uses it successfully.

End Products
- A validated job aid, performance aid, cheat sheet, performance support system, electronic performance support system, or whatever you wish to call it, and the training to teach a user how to use it

---

We didn't say much about job aids and performance tools as rapid development techniques in the chapter on OJT, which may have surprised you if you already know something about them, but I wanted to give these concepts their own chapter, as they are a rapid development shortcut that can be useful in almost any delivery process, as well as a delivery system of their own.

It doesn't matter whether you term them job aids, performance tools, performance support systems, or electronic performance support systems, at least for this discussion, as their advantages are pretty much the same when employing them as a rapid development technique. We'll call them performance aids in this chapter, just to confuse the issue a bit more.

If you are not too sure about what the differences are between these terms, you might refer once again to the companion to this book *Rapid Instructional Design*, for a quick review, or to the books in the suggested readings for a more in-depth discussion.

In general, the purpose of a performance aid is to decrease the amount of time learners spend learning, by giving them less to learn. For example, instead of memorizing a procedure, learners need only memorize how to use the performance aid that covers it and explains how to implement it.

For rapid development, this means that you will.be required to develop less learning material for the learner, at times almost none at all if the procedure is written well enough. That makes for an impressive rapid development technique.

Of course, nothing is as nice and simple as that. To use any job aid, performance tool, etc., requires some training in and of itself, and this training requires some development of learning materials. Monitored exercises where the trainee uses the performance aid are also important in learning its use. The more complicated the tool (think EPSS), the more training required to learn to use it.

This has been the basis for an error committed by many course developers, thinking that you simply present the performance aid and it takes care of itself. A performance aid that does try to achieve this goal is usually touted as having the training built in, but often isn't as effective as it might be because of this (think of some of the early software help functions that were more complicated to use than the software itself).

PERFORMANCE AIDS AS A RAPID DEVELOPMENT TECHNIQUE

At any rate, you can use performance aids to cut down on development time when they are available in the organization, or you can create them yourself, although this in turn costs you some development time. You can utilize them in most if not all of the delivery systems we've discussed previously, although you'll get the highest return (in terms of reduced development time) using them in classroom and on-the-job training deliveries. And you can use them as a delivery process all by themselves, which provides an even greater degree of rapid development, but don't forget that you will still need to develop learning materials to teach how to use the aids.

Developing the Learning Component of a Performance Aid

We've already mentioned that print self-directed learning packages are excellent candidates as a rapid development technique for the learning component of a performance aid. If you are considering an EPSS, an asynchronous e-learning package can work very well too, although, as we've discussed, the development process for these packages is much more complex.

In a distance delivery of a performance-aid-based program, a synchronous e-learning class can be a rapid development technique that works well for your learning component. For example, I recently developed a program to introduce a new series of personnel action forms to a nationwide company. There were half a dozen of them, and each had its own job aid. These formed the foundation for both the document and the training. Mostly due to time constraints, I developed a synchronous class that taught the company's HR field staff how to use the job aids, and we ran it for four weeks. By then I had developed a print self-directed learning package to take its place and train not only those we had missed with the synchronous classes, but also any new supervisors or managers who were hired.

This may not seem like much of a rapid development shortcut, as I ended up developing two learning packages for a bunch of job aids, but I used the rapid development technique of the synchronous class to meet the organization's immediate need and the advantages of the print self-directed learning package to meet the ongoing needs.

Performance aids are also great rapid development techniques when the content you need to provide is not static. It takes a lot less development time to revise a job aid and its attendant training than it does to develop an entire program. In fact, you can reduce revision time considerably in constantly changing content environments by making the performance aid the keystone of your training and then developing material around it.

RAPID DEVELOPMENT TECHNIQUES FOR DEVELOPING PERFORMANCE AIDS

So what about rapid development techniques for developing performance aids? Of course, the most effective way, as always, is to have a consultant create the performance aid for you. This is particularly true if you plan to develop an EPSS and have little or no experience doing so. These are usually fairly complicated processes and experience is paramount.

We've discussed all the advantages and disadvantages of consultants as rapid development techniques, so we won't repeat ourselves. It comes down to speed (if they have that experience we just mentioned) versus cost.

A rapid development technique for performance aids that is almost as effective, and usually much cheaper, is to find something that has already been created and either use it as is or customize it. Don't forget the training piece as well. This isn't very common though, so more often than not, you'll need to create your own performance aid.

Normally, you do this by taking the content provided through your analysis and using it to develop the performance aid. Good policies and procedures can help in your development process, but to be sure you've created a concise and complete performance aid you should depend on your analysis for the correct information. However, if you don't have an analysis or your analysis is questionable, there are other ways to develop performance aids, and some of them make for fine rapid design shortcuts.

Using Experts to Help Develop Your Performance Aids

One rapid development technique is simply to watch how an expert does it, and then create your performance aid based on your observations. Be sure you have your aid checked out carefully, both by the expert for content and nuance and by a non-expert who represents your users for usability.

A variation of this type of rapid development technique is to videotape the expert doing his or her thing, so you can replay it time and again until you are happy with the results of your performance aid. You'll still need both to validate the performance aid and to develop the training piece that will accompany it though. You might even use pieces of the video you recorded as part of your training materials for the performance aid, although this has a number of pitfalls that we won't get into here.

A simpler variation is to interview your experts, asking them what they do and why. Your notes from the interview, added to the content you've already analyzed, should make the development of your performance aid much more rapid.

You can use any combination of these rapid development techniques as well, although arguably that makes the whole process a lot less rapid. I like to use one method to develop the performance aid, and a second to validate it. For example, I often interview an expert or two when developing a job aid and then observe another expert trying to use it for validation, or to find out what I did wrong.

An even better rapid development technique for performance aids is to have the experts themselves develop them. You'll still need to validate the performance aids and learn enough about them yourself to develop the training materials that are required for them, but if you can convince someone else to do the major part of the development for you, it really is a rapid development technique, and Tom Sawyer will look down on you with a smile.

Here is a list of the most common types of performance aids that you might consider developing and using as rapid development shortcuts.

Common Types of Performance Aids

- Correctly filled-in forms
- Checklists
- Worksheets
- Photo-diagrams
- Task lists
- Conversion tables
- Graphs
- Reference books
- Step-by-step self-instruction sheets or books
- Schematic drawings
- Flow charts

Chapter 11

m-Learning and Other Delivery Systems and Rapid Development

The newest delivery system to come down the pike is mobile, or m-learning. m-Learning's major advantage is that it is true just-in-time training, available whenever and for the most part wherever the learners want it, as long as they have access to one of a number of different types of wireless devices and you, as the developer, have created the learning program in a delivery format that the wireless device can utilize.

There are a large number of disadvantages with m-learning, as there are with any new delivery technology, or old delivery technology as far as that goes, and this isn't the place to discuss them, but for the developer they are mostly related to bandwidth, storage capability, screen size, and the fact that cell phones, iPods, and the BlackBerry were not created with training in mind.

However, these disadvantages create rapid development opportunities such as pod-casts, and cell-phone-capable programs do not allow for much in the way of developing time-consuming media or extensive interactions. Now you might say, "Wait a minute, isn't that the tail wagging the dog?" How can it be a rapid development technique if you can't develop material because of the limitations of the delivery system?" That's a good question, and I don't have a good answer as a developer. The only likely one lies more in design.

As a designer, you choose the most effective delivery process available, then as a developer you take advantage of the strengths of that process and try to reduce the effects of its weaknesses. If the design decision was to use some form of m-learning as the delivery system, for whatever good reasons, a first-rate developer will develop material that fits it, not try to shoehorn in materials that don't. This in itself is a rapid development technique. Know what your m-delivery can support and what it can't, and develop material accordingly. It will save you time and frustration.

One of the advantages of m-learning is that the hardware is inexpensive, and sometimes free, as many employees have cell phones, MP3 players, and other mobile devices. If you are in a small company that can't afford another type of distributed learning system due to the cost, m-learning may be your only choice, and so you design and develop material for it.

m-Learning can be an excellent delivery system for an EPSS or a simple electronic job aid, which makes these processes possible rapid development techniques when combined with an m-delivery. It has even been around long enough for consultants to have created m-learning-specific templates and authoring software, which in turn become rapid development techniques for the development of m-learning.

Another rapid development technique that works well with m-learning is to record presentations that are given for various reasons by various people in the organization, edit them, and add objectives, then make them available as pod-casts. An amazing amount of information in at least a somewhat systematic format can be distributed this way with limited material development.

We discussed the rapid development advantages of informal learning earlier, that is, learning where the learner is responsible for deciding some or all of the aspects of the learning. m-Learning is quickly becoming the delivery system for this type of learning, with discussion forums, online communities, Wikis, and blogs, all delivered through mobile hardware, providing for complete self-direction in learning, or simply places for focused learning discussions to happen.

RAPID DEVELOPMENT TECHNIQUES FOR DEVELOPING SIMULATIONS

Simulations come in all different shapes and sizes, from simple paper processes such as a role play to multi-player electronic learning games that can take hours and even days to complete. There are branching stories, mini-games, interactive spread sheets, and virtual labs.

The best rapid development technique for simulations, no matter how simple or complex they are, is one we've discussed before, buy 'em, buy 'em, buy 'em. Find already developed simulations and either use them as is or modify them for your needs. This is particularly true for higher-level simulations, as they take great amounts of time to develop and even more to validate.

The second-best rapid development technique for simulations is to utilize consultants who know what they're doing and who have had plenty of experience in the art to develop your simulation. I consider this second-best, as you do need to spend development time working with the consultants and overseeing their work, no matter how good they are, and the cost is often prohibitive.

If you must create your own simulations from scratch, there are few really effective rapid development techniques that I can think of. The best advice I can give you is to read a good book or two on the process (see the suggested readings list), and try to keep your simulation as simple as possible while still allowing your learners to get what they need from it.

Recently some simulation development tools have come on the market. These can be a rapid development shortcut if they are related to the content you are working on and they are not too difficult to learn, which is usually the problem with all new technology development tools.

One of the fastest-growing classes of simulations are those used for soft skills such as role playing, problem solving, and business modeling. Like all simulations, these can be very time-consuming to build from scratch, but a number of template-based simulation tools do exist for these types of simulations. Examples of these are Experience Builder from ExperienceBuilders, Redwood Development Platform from Redwood e-learning systems, and Simulated Role Play from SIMmersion.

There are also technical skills simulations that model various machinery and systems or act as task simulators such as a flight simulator. They can be used in your program for troubleshooting and diagnostics, procedural walkthroughs or situational simulations. Once again, vendors such as NGRAIN and Knowledge Dynamics can supply you with development tools that work well as rapid development shortcuts for these types of simulations.

REUSABLE CONTENT OBJECTS AS A RAPID DEVELOPMENT SHORTCUT

I've sort of saved the best for last as far as rapid development techniques are concerned. The concept of reusable content objects has been around for a while now. It has gone through a number of transformations, but its basic premise hasn't changed—developing small slugs of content, with all the materials and media that are associated with them, and then reusing them when they are applicable for other programs. You can't get a much more rapid development technique than this. Theoretically, if you had a large enough library of reusable content objects, you could create entire programs with little or no development at all, just by combining blocks together and adding some transitions.

Of course, this is more a dream than a goal, but you can certainly utilize reusable content objects to decrease your development time when you are creating a course that has similar content to one you've already developed.

Developing Reusable Content Objects the First Time

The main drawback of reusable content objects is the time and planning it takes to do their primary development. You need to use a consistent development template for every content block so that it can be utilized in other programs that you create later with the same development template and, of course, the same delivery system.

This has not worked well when attempted across multiple organizations. Every company has its own development process and a way it prefers its end-products to look. Even though reusable content objects should be at a more granular level, and therefore not affected by style, this is seldom the case.

For some time now, reusable content object fans, particularly vendors, have been trying to drive the reusable content object down to a level where style doesn't matter, but they've met with limited to no success. At such a level the reusable content object tends to lose much of its efficiency and become little more than an objective with a piece of content attached.

Most vendors have more or less given up on the dream of banks of properly developed reusable content objects that they could sell to their clients, overwhelmed by their client organizations' need to have it "their way."

However, within an organization, standardization of development templates is more than possible. It is often required. Therefore, home-grown reusable content objects that a developer can create for one program, then bank for use in other programs, are very possible. For example, the basic skills required for making presentations; audience awareness, listening skills, non-verbal behaviors, etc., are the same for trainers, team leaders, and executives. In one company I worked with, we created reusable content objects for each of these, with all the associated media and activities, when we were developing a train-the-trainer session. We used these reusable content objects later for a program on platform presentation techniques for managers, and later still in a course for supervisors on leading meetings. One development, three programs! You can't get much more rapid than that!

KNOWLEDGE MANAGEMENT AS A RAPID DEVELOPMENT TECHNIQUE

If training is the transfer of knowledge, then knowledge management is a form of training delivery and an incredible rapid development technique, as you need to do no development at all... sort of.

There are any number of knowledge management schemes in use, but like reusable content objects, they have as their foundation a single concept; Find a way to make learnings that occur in an organization accessible to everyone across the organization who can take advantage of them, so we don't keep continuously reinventing the wheel because we lost or were unable to distribute new organizational knowledge. For example, a telecom company I worked for put into place a knowledge management system related to customer problem solving. Every time the engineering department solved a customer problem, the problem and solution were entered into a database. The software for the system kept a key word file based on each entry, and if another engineering group had a customer problem they went to the database, entered the key words closest to their problem, and scanned for results. More often than not, their customer's problem, or something very close to it, had been solved by some other group in the organization, or at the very least there were some common aspects that could be employed to keep them from having to solve the problem from scratch.

So... what the heck does this have to do with rapid development? Basically, a knowledge management system that is well designed and consistently used will reduce the need for you to train and, of course, therefore to develop training materials. I expect you already figured that out, but I thought I'd better say it anyway.

Knowledge management systems are their own training delivery, simply by transferring knowledge from one part of the organization to the other. Any that you have or create are by their nature rapid development shortcuts.

Because you've come this far in this book, you probably have enough of an understanding of rapid development techniques by now to realize that a knowledge management system is basically a performance tool, and you are aware that, as with all performance tools, you need to train the organization on how to use it if it is to function effectively. However, the development time spent doing this is significantly less than the time you would have spent developing the numerous training programs that the knowledge management system eliminates the need for.

There is another aspect to a knowledge management system that might affect you as a developer, or at least as a trainer, and that is that monitoring of it is required to make sure your learners are using it effectively, particularly inputting the stuff that needs to be input. This does take time and usually falls on the shoulders of the people who recommended the knowledge management process to begin with—very often, you.

So knowledge management as a rapid development technique is not really a free ride; it does require development time invested in the training, and time in the monitoring as well, but even so, it can still save you plenty of development time when used properly.

RAPID DEVELOPMENT OF BETA TESTS AND PILOTS

Off and on throughout this book we've mentioned planning for and completing beta tests and pilots. Like train-the-trainer processes, these aspects of course development are sometimes included in the development phase and sometimes in the implementation phase. I like them better in the development phase, so let's discuss them a bit in relation to their rapid development techniques.

In case you've forgotten, you run a beta test to see how the pieces of your course hold together and whether they work as a whole. Betas are also used to isolate (in a controlled environment) particular aspects of your course that you are not totally sure of, such as special activities, laboratories, complex simulations, and so forth. The importance of a beta test is that it is usually the first time you will receive feedback from a live audience concerning your course and its component parts.

For a *beta test*, your audience should include a few representative trainees and an SME or two to give you their viewpoint on the material. If you can, invite another instructional designer for an instructional design review as well. In an extensive beta you might also include the managers or supervisors of your target trainees, other training stakeholders, and anyone else you can round up to fill out the audience.

A *pilot*, on the other hand, is run within the exact parameters and in the exact environment in which you run the actual classes. The purpose of the pilot is to make sure the class will work just as you designed it to, when you deliver it for real. A pilot allows you to evaluate things that a beta test does not. Timing is one of these things. You don't stop to garner feedback during a pilot, so you can check whether a two-day class can be run in two days and whether a one-hour activity takes one hour. Logistics should also be assessed during a pilot, which is why you always run a pilot in the actual training environment.

Your pilot should run just a bit longer than your training normally will when you roll it out. The slight additional time is for a post-program debriefing and feedback session. Otherwise, if it's a two-day training session, the pilot should last two days.

Also, the audience for your pilot is different. Gone are the managers, instructional designers, and others who were part of the beta. Your audience for the pilot is the trainees intended for your program—and in the same numbers as your program will support when you roll it out. Here is a quick comparison of beta tests to pilots.

Beta Test	**Pilot**
Stop at any point	Must run straight through
Can observe and interact	No direct observation
Questions can be asked during	Questions at end only
Can prepare learners orally	Must be done cold
Program in draft format	Program basically finalized
Different audiences	Target audience only
Time is double	Time is slightly more
Can do all in one room	Must do in learning environment
Tests content	Tests implementation, flow, time

Rapid Development Shortcuts for Beta Tests

A number of techniques can be employed to cut down on the amount of time you spend doing beta testing. One of the simplest is not to do it at all. I don't recommend this, but when time is of the essence this is one area where you can skimp a bit. You make up for not having a beta test in the pilot, which means your pilot debriefing needs to be longer and more complete, and it also means you may need to do more rework than you normally would after a pilot, but betas take a lot of time and the rework seldom comes close to that number of hours.

This isn't true in asynchronous e-learning, where the re-work can be incredibly time-consuming and expensive. Don't skimp on your beta test here; you'll more than pay for it later.

Another rapid development shortcut for beta testing is only to test those areas that you need to test, that is, activities, labs, and other aspects that have the highest probability of causing problems when the program is rolled out. Once again, the pilot can take up the slack for those areas you did not beta test.

In this approach, or any beta test plan, be sure to create strong, focused questions for your participants to answer. This will not only give you the information you need, but will save the participants time trying to figure our what you are looking for, as well as your time trying to wade through a lot of commentary to get to the important information. Questions such as "What did you like and dislike about the program?" often lead to a lot of discussion about things that are not relevant to the material, such as policies and procedures the learners don't like, or even discussions of why the course is even being given. I try to stay away from these types of open-ended questions; in fact, lately I've been eliminating the verbal debriefing completely, relying on my written questions to give me what I need to know.

One of the other problems with oral debriefings is that one or two individuals with an axe to grind tend to take over, and the others don't get a chance to speak. Sending the questions out ahead of time, particularly to SMEs who have helped with parts of the program already, will save even more time and further decrease wasted effort.

In asynchronous development, a rapid prototyping model can be used for this shortcut, prototyping the more complex aspects of your program as individual pieces and doing beta tests on those pieces before you assemble the whole and do the pilot.

When holding a classic "walk-through" beta test, shorten the time you'll need to spend analyzing the data by having someone else do the facilitation while you (as the developer) sit and take notes. If this isn't possible, be sure to find a colleague, preferably one who knows at least something about the program and program development, to take notes for you while you teach. Shorten train-the-trainer time and get a better read on how easy it is for your trainers to use your instructor guides by having one of them teach the beta.

You can also reduce the time you spend in beta testing in a classroom, OJT, or synchronous delivery setting by doing it in a focus group style, rather than as a walk-through. Bring your beta participants together, have them read your material (don't expect them to read it ahead of time, as most won't, and you'll waste the time of those who do waiting for the others to catch up), and then let them "have at it." Use a tape recorder to catch all their comments, as you'll be too busy listening and asking questions to be taking notes as well

Or, instead of a full "walk-through," do a "talk-through" in which you talk to your beta participants as a focus group throughout the program, stopping to focus on those aspects you feel are key or that you are unsure about. Any of these approaches will save you plenty of development time when teamed with a strong pilot.

Rapid Development Shortcuts for Pilots

Because the pilot is basically a final review of the program as it will be implemented, there are not a lot of rapid development shortcuts that you can use. The best I can think of is to do a solid beta test. If you've done your beta well, you should have few problems in the pilot and few necessary revisions after it, just some adjustments to the timing of the various parts. As with beta testing, having a set of strong, focused questions, and not "What did you like?" types for discussion at the end of the pilot, can help you isolate any problems the beta test might have missed.

One possible timesaver, although it saves more implementation time than development time, is to do a live pilot, that is, a pilot that is actually the first iteration of the program. Once again, a strong beta test before this is attempted is an excellent idea; otherwise you can easily find yourself needing to retrain the learners you just trained after you fixed the things that didn't work. Be sure that the participants know they are part of a pilot so that, if some things don't go quite as planned, they'll give you and your program the benefit of the doubt.

RAPID BETA TESTS AND PILOTS FOR OTHER DELIVERY FORMATS

Most of the rapid development techniques for beta tests and pilots that we've discussed so far are more related to classroom or OJT types of deliveries, although some are applicable to synchronous e-learning as well. We also mentioned a few techniques for asynchronous e-learning beta tests that will work for print self-directed learning programs as well.

One shortcut we didn't mention that is useful for any form of self-instruction, particularly if it is in a distributed setting, is to have all of your beta participants in one room for the beta testing. This makes asking them questions much more efficient and effective, and also allows you to give them directions for focusing in on key issues. We've already discussed how this will save you time in analyzing the beta test data as well. Remember though that this is a good development shortcut for a beta test, not a pilot. Pilots, especially self-instructional pilots in distributed implementations, must be run in the environment, and exactly as they will be run when your programs go out to your learners.

For the other delivery methods we've discussed in this book, there are very few beta test shortcuts, and even fewer pilot ones. Because of the complexity of blended approaches and the individuality of structure mentoring deliveries, you may be able to use a few of the minor concepts we discussed, such as creating well-focused questions and using note-takers, in specific instances, but for the most part you will need to run your beta tests and pilots without shortcuts to obtain the information you need.

Here are a few general but focused questions you might ask during your beta test and/or pilot to shorten the amount of time you spend analyzing data:

- Are all of the objectives clear and complete for the learners?
- Are all terms properly defined?
- Is the important content stressed enough?
- Are the learner evaluations sufficient?
- Were the learners able to meet the objectives?
- Are the directions to the learners clear and complete?
- Is the pacing correct?
- Is the overview adequate?
- Is the sequence of material logical?
- Are the learner benefits explained in enough detail?
- Is the content relevant to the learners?
- Are practice sessions implemented where needed and with correct timing?
- Is there sufficient feedback for the learners?
- Are activities sufficient and timely?
- Are transitions comfortable?
- Are there adequate reviews and summaries?
- Is the media appropriate and effective?

- Is the reading level appropriate for the audience?
- Was the participation adequate?

To summarize much of what we have discussed in this book, here is a chart that shows the major delivery systems and some of their most important associated rapid development techniques, along with a few comments to help remind you what you've learned about them.

A SUMMARY OF MAJOR RAPID DEVELOPMENT TECHNIQUES BY DELIVERY SYSTEM

Delivery System	RDT	Effective Savings	Comments
Classroom	Develop instructor guides to match your instructors' requirements	High	Watch for SMEs who are not really SMEs
	Use templates for your instructor guides	Medium	
	Include only information that will be used in the class in your participant package	High	Stay away from nice-to-know material
	Create a template for use when developing participant packages	Medium	Be sure to include style information
			Don't forget a place for the objectives
	Use your hard-copy PowerPoint slides as passouts	Medium	Stops you from giving away the answers
			Make it easy for your learners to integrate them into their participant package
	Borrow classroom activities from other sources	High	Be careful with copyright
	Prepare your classroom instructors at a distance	Medium	Save travel time
	Create your own "official" template for PowerPoint slides	Medium	Keep animations and clip art only to those that enhance the learning
	Use flip charts to create interactions instead of developing them	Medium	Prepare all or part of your flip chart in advance
	Do videos in slugs	Medium	Edit pre-made videos into slugs too for multiple uses

On-the-Job Training	Refer to operating and tech manuals, don't include them in your learning guide	Medium	Make your directions for their use to both learners and instructors very clear
	Use outdated equipment to set up OJT labs	High	This RDT works well when regular equipment is being used 24/7 and saves you from creating simulations
	Use SMEs for more than just instruction	High	Discuss the development with them
			Observe them before developing
Asynchronous e-Learning	Customize an off-the-shelf program	High	Can be done by you or vendor
			Be careful of copyright
	Rapid prototyping	High	Chose the rapid prototyping concept that will work best for your situation
	Hire consultants	High	For entire program or just for specialties such as programming activities
			Be sure they are experienced
	Scripts and storyboards	Medium	Do them and keep them simple
	Repurpose classroom activities	Low	Chose those that will work and don't try to force the others
	Repurpose video	Medium	Create video in "slugs"
	Use authoring tools and systems	Medium	Takes time to learn but saves it in the end
			Better for new developers
Synchronous e-Learning	Repurpose stand-up classes	Medium	Chose classes that have characteristics amenable to a synchronous delivery
	Repurpose classroom activities	Medium	Look for activities from a variety of sources
	Borrow ideas from others	Medium	See what your software vendor has that you can use
	Know your facilitators	Medium	Decrease the complexity of your facilitator guide if your facilitators are seasoned synchronous instructors

	Use your SMEs well	High	Have them available during the class to answer questions
			Have them teach part of class
			Put them in debates and panel discussions
	Train your trainers by making them class participants	High	Both cost and time efficient and very effective.
			Have them teach a section or two with you before going it alone
	Use chat rooms and discussion boards	High	Develop your questions or problems carefully
			Provide a final posting of expert thoughts on the question at hand
Online Learning	Hold a synchronous first class	Medium	Saves a small amount of development time but plenty of travel time
	Use learning contracts as a foundation	High	Focuses purely on learners' needs
			Requires a good template and strong monitoring
	Use online as a RDT for other deliveries	High	Works well with both synchronous and asynchronous deliveries.
			Can take the place of some face-to-face classroom delivery
Blended Learning	Use blended as a RDT for other deliveries	High	Blends of classroom and OJT, asynchronous and classroom, or synchronous and asynchronous are common and very effective
	Blend synchronous and asynchronous to utilize your group classroom activities when repurposing a face-to-face classroom	Medium	Your other classroom activities will translate better and quicker in the synchronous aspect as well
			This is the ultimate in travel cost savings combined with maximum learning effectiveness

Structured Mentoring	Utilize off-the-shelf videos or asynchronous programs	Medium	Be sure to create debriefing discussion questions for the mentor and the trainee to use
Self-Directed Learning	Create an SDL package to accompany asynchronous e-learning	Medium	Provides a different learning modality
			Create entire programs using this approach
			Consider using in conjunction with PowerPoint presentations
	Institute an individualized prescriptive employee development initiative	High	Utilize learning contracts
			Develop or purchase asynchronous course libraries
Performance Aids	Use them as an RDT	High	Works well in environments in which content is quickly changing
			Don't forget training on using the performance aid
	Hire a consultant to help you create your electronic performance support system	High	Be sure the consultant is experienced in EPSS development
	Observe/videotape/ interview an expert	Medium	Have your performance aid reviewed by the expert and piloted by a representative user
			Don't forget training on using the performance aid.
Mobile Learning	Know what your mobile learning process will support and develop material accordingly.	High	
	Develop pod-casts from presentations given in the organization	Medium	Tape them, edit them, and add objectives

Suggested Resources

Classroom

Foshay, R., Silber, K.H., & Stelnicki, M. (2003). *Writing training materials that work: How to train anyone to do anything*. San Francisco, CA: Pfeiffer.

Pike, B. (1994). *Creative training techniques handbook* (2nd ed.). Minneapolis, MN: Lakewood.

Piskurich, G.M. (2005). *Classroom facilitation: The art and the science*. Bellevue, KY: MicroPress.

e-Learning (Asynchronous)

Adams, D. (1997, May/June). What's the story? Creating and using story boards. *CBT Solutions*, pp. 36–40.

Allen, M. (2003). *Michael Allen's guide to e-learning*. Hoboken, NJ: John Wiley & Sons.

Computer Training Network: www.thectn.com/

Conrad, K. (2000). *Instructional design for web-based training*. Amherst, MA: Human Resource Development Press.

Cross, J., & Dublin, L. (2002). *Implementing e-learning*. Alexandria, VA: ASTD.

Driscoll, M. (1997, April). Defining internet-based and web-based training. *Performance Improvement*, pp. 5–7.

Henderson, A. (2003). *The e-learning question and answer book*. New York: AMACOM.

145

Horton, W. (2000). *Designing web-based training: How to teach anyone anything anywhere anytime.* Hoboken, NJ: John Wiley & Sons.

Horton, W., & Horton, K. (2003). *Tools and technologies for e-learning: A consumer's guide for trainers, teachers, educators, and instructional designers.* Hoboken, NJ: John Wiley & Sons.

Mantyla, K. (2001). *Blending e-learning.* Alexandria, VA: ASTD.

Piskurich, G. (Ed.). (2003). *Preparing learners for e-learning.* San Francisco, CA: Pfeiffer.

Piskurich, G. (Ed.). (2003). *The AMA handbook of e-learning.* New York: AMACOM.

Rosenberg, M. (2001). *e-Learning.* New York: McGraw-Hill.

Schank, R. (2002). *Designing world-class e-learning.* New York: McGraw-Hill.

The Masie Center: www.masie.com

Write successful video scripts. *Info-Line,* 8707. Alexandria, VA: ASTD.

www.bnhexpertsoft.com/english/products/advent/overview.htm

www.brandonhallnews.com

www.intrack.com/intranet/

e-Learning (Synchronous)

Distance learning software: http://ilinc.com

Goldsmith, J.J. (1999). Development teams for creating technology-based training. In G. M. Piskurich (Ed.), *The ASTD handbook of training design and delivery.* Alexandria, VA: ASTD.

Hanna, D. (2003). *147 practical tips for teaching online groups.* New York: Atwood.

Hofmann, J. (2001). *The synchronous trainer's survival guide.* Hertfordshire, UK: InSync Training Synergy, LLC.

Mantyla, K. (1998). *Interactive distance learning activities that really work.* Alexandria, VA: ASTD.

Online meeting center: www.webex.com

Piskurich, G. (2004). *Getting the most from online learning.* San Francisco, CA: Pfeiffer.

Stewart, J. (1999, May). Synchronous distance learning: The interactive internet classroom. *CBT Solutions,* pp. 25–28.

Games and Activities

10 great games and how to use them. *Info-Line,* 411. Alexandria, VA: ASTD.

Kirk, J., & Belovics, R. (2004). An intoduction to online learning games. *Learning Circuits.*

Newstrom, J. (1980). *Games trainers play.* New York: McGraw-Hill.

Newstrom, J. (1989). *More games trainers play.* New York: McGraw-Hill.

Silberman, M. (1996). *Active training: A handbook of techniques, designs, case examples, and tips.* San Francisco, CA: Pfeiffer.

Sugar, S. (1999). *Games that teach.* San Francisco, CA: Pfeiffer.

Thiagi *GamesLetter*: www.thiagi.com

Thiagi's home page: www.thiagi.com/index.html

Underwood, T. (1996). *Wuzzle book.* Minneapolis, MN: Resources for Organizations.

www.games2train.com

www.presentersuniversity.com

Instructional Design

ASTD: www.astd.org/

Basics of instructional design. *Info-Line,* 803. Alexandria, VA: ASTD.

Chapman, B.L. (1995). Accelerating the instructional design process: A tool for instructional designers. *Journal of Interactive Instruction Development, 8*(2).

Dick, W., & Carey, L. (1990). *The systematic design of instruction* (3rd ed.). New York: HarperCollins.

Don Clark (alias Big Dog): www.nwlink.com/~donclark/hrd.html

Gayeski, D. (1998, April). Out of the box instructional design. *Training & Development, 52*(4).

Hodell, C. (2000). *ISD from the ground up.* Alexandria, VA: ASTD.

ISPI: www.ispi.org/

Piskurich, G. (2003). *Trainer basics.* Alexandria, VA: ASTD.

Piskurich, G. (2006). *Rapid instructional design* (2nd ed.) (2006). San Francisco, CA: Pfeiffer.

Job Aids and Performance Support Systems

Basics of electronic performance support systems. *Info-Line,* 9412. Alexandria, VA: ASTD.

Gery, G. (1991). *Electronic performance support systems.* New York: Ziff Instate Publishers.

Making EPSS work for your organization. *Info-Line,* 9501. Alexandria, VA: ASTD.

McFarland, R. (n.d.). *Expert systems in education and training.* Englewood Cliffs, NJ: Educational Technology Publications.

Miller, B. (1999, April). On-line help supports performance. *Performance Improvement,* pp. 32–35.

Mitchell, D. (1993, May/June). On using job aids in lieu of or as an adjunct to training. *Performance & Instruction,* pp. 32–33.

Nelson, J. (1989). Quick and dirty job aids. *Performance & Instruction, 28,* 35–36.

Rossett, A. (1994). *A handbook of job aids.* San Francisco, CA: Pfeiffer.

Ruyle, K. (1991, February/March). *Developing intelligent job aids intelligently. Technical and Skills Training,* pp. 25–28.

Stevens, E. (1995). *Designing electronic performance support tools.* Englewood Cliffs, NJ: Educational Technology Publications.

Tilaro, A. (1998, October). Creating motivating job aids. *Performance & Instruction,* pp. 13–20.

Williams, S.W. (1999). Performance support systems and job aids. In G.M. Piskurich (Ed.), *The ASTD handbook of training design and delivery.* Alexandria, VA: ASTD.

Knowledge Management

Chawla, S., & Renesch, J. (Eds.) (1995). *Learning organizations: Developing cultures for tomorrow's workplace.* Florence, KY: Productivity Press.

Davenport, T., & Prusak, L. (1997). *Working knowledge: How organizations manage what they know.* Cambridge, MA: Harvard Business School Press.

Marquardt, M.J. (2002). *Building the learning organization.* Palo Alto, CA: Davies-Black.

Nonaka, I., & Takeuchi, H. (1995). *The knowledge creating company: How Japanese companies create the dynamics of innovation.* London: Oxford University Press.

Rossett, A. (1999). Knowledge management meets analysis. *Training & Development, 53*(5).

Rumizen, M. (2001). *The complete idiot's guide to knowledge management.* New York: Alpha Books.

Senge, P. (1994). *The fifth discipline: The art and practice of learning.* New York: Currency/Doubleday.

On-the-Job Training

Gallup, D.A. (1999). On-the-job training. In G.M. Piskurich (Ed.), *The ASTD handbook of training design and delivery.* Alexandria, VA: ASTD.

Jacobs, R. (1990). *Structured on-the-job training.* San Francisco, CA: Berrett-Koehler.

Mager, E. (1999, February). The instructor coach. *Performance Improvement,* pp. 26–31.

Pike, B. (1999). *One-on-one training: How to effectively train one person at a time.* San Francisco, CA: Pfeiffer.

Semb, G. (1995). On-the-job training prescriptions and practice. *Performance Improvement Quarterly, 8,* 19–37.

Tyson, L. (1993). Designing on-the-job training. In *The ASTD handbook of instructional technology.* Alexandria, VA: ASTD.

Media

Anderson, R., & Reynolds, A. (1992). *Selecting and developing media for instruction* (3rd ed.). New York: Van Nostrand Reinhold.

Brandt, R. (1986). *Flip charts: How to draw them and use them.* San Francisco, CA: Pfeiffer.

King, B. (1993). Applying graphic design principles. In *The ASTD handbook of instructional technology.* Alexandria, VA: ASTD.

Parker, E. (1999, April). Making instructional design readable. *Performance & Instruction,* pp. 26–27.

Write, design, and produce effective training materials. *Info-Line,* 508. Alexandria, VA: ASTD.

Wilder, C. (2002). *Point, Click, & Wow!* San Francisco, CA: Pfeiffer.

Online Learning

American Center for the Study of Distance Learning: www.cde.psu.edu/acsde

Blount, R. (2002). How to build an e-learning community. *E-learning,* 2, 18–23.

Distance Learning: The Virtual University Gazette: www.geteducated.com/vugaz.htm

Mantyla, K., & Gividen, J. (1997). *Distance learning.* Alexandria, VA: ASTD.

Palloff, R., & Pratt, K. (2001). *Lessons from the cyberspace classroom.* San Francisco, CA: Jossey-Bass.

The Distance Education Clearinghouse: www.uwex.edu/disted

USDLA: www.usdla.org

www.distance-educator.com

www.onlinelearningmag.com

Rapid Prototyping

Stokes, J.T., & Richey, R.C. (2000). Rapid prototyping methodology in action: A developmental study. *Educational Technology and Development,* 48(2), 63–80.

Tripp, S.D. (1990). Rapid prototyping. *Educational Technology Research and Development,* 38(1), 31–44.

www.kmsi.us/white_paper05.htm

www-personal.umich.edu/~jmargeru/prototyping/

Reusable Learning Objects

Hathway, A. (1998, January/February). Reusable content objectives. *CBT Solutions,* pp. 26–39.

Merrill, D. (1998, March/April). Knowledge objects. *CBT Solutions,* pp. 1–11.

Wiley, D. (2002). *The instructional use of learning objects.* Bloomington, IN: Agency for Instructional Technology.

Self-Directed Learning

Hatcher, T.G. (1997, Febuary). The ins and outs of self-directed learning. *Training & Development.*

Piskurich, G.M. (1993). *Self-directed learning.* San Francisco, CA: Jossey-Bass.

Simulations

Chapman, B., & Hall, B. (2007). *Online simulations 2007: A knowledge base of 100+ simulation development tools and services.* Sunnyvale CA. Brandon Hall Research.

Lierman, B. (1993). Designing laboratory and simulation instruction. In *The ASTD handbook of instructional technology.* New York: McGraw-Hill.

Sources for Vendors

Biech, E. (2005). Using off-the-shelf training. In *Training for dummies.* Hoboken, NJ: John Wiley & Sons.

Cowan, S.L. (2000). Outsourcing training. *Info-Line.* Alexandria, VA: ASTD.

Field, T. (1997). An outsourcing buyers' guide caveat emptor. *CIO* magazine.

Nantel, R., Vipond, S., & Hall, B. (2007). *Authoring tool knowledgebase 2007: A buyer's guide to 105+ of the best e-learning content development applications.* Sunnyvale, CA: Brandon Hall Research.

Vendors (Development Software)

www.adobe.com
www.allencomm.com
www.articulate.com
www.bnhexpertsoft.com/english/products/advent/overview.htm
www.SDLGlobal.com
www.macromedia.com

Glossary

Active Performance Support System: An electronic performance support system that actually monitors the employees' work and stops them to lend advice and support when necessary. There are few of these in existence.

Alpha Test: The first evaluation of a technology-based program, used to test the user interface and to determine overall usability.

Analog Audio and Video: Audio or video information normally stored in a tape format; it is differentiated from digital audio and video, which usually use some type of computer format as the storage medium. Digital video and audio are needed for e-learning and CD-ROM training deliveries.

Animation: A sequence of graphics presented in succession, animation is widely used to simulate motion in computer-based or e-learning deliveries.

Aspect Ratio: The relationship of height to width of an image size (for example, 4:3 is a standard aspect ratio for NTSC television).

ASTD: an organization of training professionals encompassing all aspects of the profession. Believe it or not ASTD is no longer the American Society for Training and Development it is just ASTD.

Asynchronous: Usually in reference to e-learning, asynchronous refers to non-instructor-led training using a computer-network-based delivery system in which the trainees are not online at the same time nor in direct, immediate contact. The technique sometimes includes the use of electronic bulletin boards and chat rooms. It is often a mixed-media format combining a self-instructional aspect with one or more instructor-facilitated processes.

Audience Analysis: An evaluation of a training audience to determine the background, needs, interests, preferences, and demographics of the group.

Authoring System: A software application used to create courseware by combining text, graphics, video, audio, and animations.

Bandwidth: Technically a concept that has to do with the size of the wire that connects computers in a network and how much information can flow over it. Usually the more bandwidth the better, as more information can be sent faster.

Beta Test: An evaluation for a course or product, done by actual users and others, not necessarily in a real-life environment, to determine instructional flow and answer questions that surfaced during development of materials. It is also referred to as a *formative evaluation*, although this term is being used less frequently.

Brainstorming: A technique for idea generation in which each person suggests as many ideas as possible, with no discussion of viability until after the session is complete. A recorder usually writes the ideas on some medium for this later discussion.

Branch Back: A technique whereby a wrong answer causes the program to replay the area of instruction where the correct answer resides.

Branching: An instructional technique in which the learner's next step is determined by his or her response to a previous step. Branching makes a course more interactive by allowing students to take different paths through a course, based on their needs and interests.

Browser: A software program that allows trainees to navigate through a web-based training program.

Bug: A programming error that causes a course to run improperly or stop running unexpectedly. Alpha tests are used to find bugs. Bugs are also known by the euphemism *undocumented features*, although usually only by programmers.

Bulletin Board: Software that allows trainees to post class information, activities, or questions electronically for reading by other participants, the instructor, or both.

CBT (see Computer-Based Training).

CD-ROM: A delivery technology for multimedia-based programs. It is used mostly for self-instructional training designs. It has some compatibility and storage size problems.

Chat Room: An electronic "place" where individuals can connect by sending typed text to one another in real time.

Checklist: A tool used to ensure that the important actions or steps in the performance of a task have been taken.

Chunking: The process of dividing a portion of training material into smaller pieces that are easier to deal with.

Color Scheme: A group of complementary colors used in computer-based training to give a course a consistent look.

Competency: The specific knowledge and skills and the application of that knowledge and those skills to the standard of performance required for a particular job.

Completion Item: A test item requiring the completion of a statement, phrase, or concept.

Compressed File: Files that are reduced in size to allow for quicker transfer and more efficient storage. Particularly used by audio and video files across computer nets.

Computer-Based Training (CBT): Can be a general term for any training done through the use of computers rather than through instructor facilitation, but is also often used to signify only text-based computer-facilitated instruction. This is usually referred to derogatorily as an "electronic page turner" and is not considered good instruction.

Content: The concepts, ideas, policies, and information that a training program comprises.

Content Outline: An outline that organizes course content into topics and subtopics.

Cost-Benefit Analysis: A method of assigning dollar values to the cost of training development and implementation and to the benefits derived from the training, to determine whether it is worth the effort.

Course: A complete, usually integrated series of lessons identified by a common title. Courses usually make up a training curriculum, and in turn are made up of modules, units, sections, and so forth.

Course Map: The major concepts from a course depicted in a visual arrangement, usually with lines drawn between associated concepts and relationships shown between the connected concepts. Maps usually break the course into units, lessons, frames, or segments, and they detail objectives, treatment, teaching strategies, and a skeleton storyboard if needed.

Courseware: The media (text, computer program, CD-ROM, and so on) that contains the content of the course.

Criterion-Referenced Testing: Testing of the objectives as a learner progresses through the course of instruction. Success depends on the trainees' attainment of the objectives and *not* on how well they do in relation to others.

Cross-Training: Providing training in several different areas or functions. This provides backup workers when the primary worker is unavailable.

Design Document: A conceptual report that gives all those involved in the development of a training program a picture of the overall course design. Items might include a mission statement, an audience profile, course objectives, content outline, a course map, an evaluation plan, and a visual motif.

Designer: An individual who attempts to make it easier for learners to learn by systematically discovering what a learner needs to know and then determining the best way to make that information available.

Desktop Training: Any training delivered by computer to a trainee's desk.

Dial-Up Connection: Using a modem and telephone line to connect to a computer net.

Digital Audio: Audio information stored as discrete numeric values. Computer disks, digital audiotape (DAT), and CD-ROMs are typical storage media for both digital audio and video.

Digital Video: Video that is digitized on a computer instead of residing on a magnetic tape. Digital video is easier to store, edit, and play on a computer. This also makes it more expensive, and it takes up large amounts of storage capacity.

Digital Versatile Disc (DVD): DVD is a delivery technology that allows full motion video and all the other goodies of multimedia on a small-sized disc with plenty of storage capacity.

Digitize: To store media (graphic, audio, or video) in digital form. Often used to note the conversion from an analog to a digital format.

Distance Learning: Probably one of the most overused and much-abused terms in technology-based training. At the basic level it simply means that the instructor and the learner are either not in the same physical location or not there at the same time, or both. However, it is often used to refer to satellite-mediated learning, even though computers, video players, and even telephones can be used as distance-learning delivery systems.

Distributed Implementation: A self-instructional delivery process in which there is no designated learning center. The packages are sent to the trainees' job locations and usually facilitated by a supervisor or other line individual.

Distributed Learning: A newer and also older term that means roughly the same thing as distance learning, but is coming into use due to distance learning's perceived relationship with satellites.

Download: To receive and store information from another computer or system.

Drill-and-Practice Exercises: Instructional activities designed to allow a learner to review previously learned information through repetition and rehearsal. Often a major activity set for computer-based training.

DVD (see Digital Versatile Disc).

e-Learning: Technology-based training using the Internet as the delivery system. Advantages of this delivery system include reduced hardware compatibility issues, easier and quicker revisions, and the possible maximum size of the distribution network. The disadvantages include security problems, speed, and bandwidth limitations, which reduce multimedia capability. e-Learning can be instructor-led or self-directed.

Electronic Performance Support System (EPSS): Computerized applications that provide support for the user in accomplishing specific tasks, particularly those that are difficult to memorize or are done infrequently. An electronic performance support system may provide needed information, present job aids, and deliver just-in-time training on demand. Electronic performance support systems will often take the place of some training, although the employees need to be trained on how to use the system effectively.

Entry Skills (Entry Behavior): Skills or knowledge that the trainee must master before he or she can begin a training program.

EPSS (see Electronic Performance Support System).

Evaluation: Reviewing a course to determine its impact and improve its effectiveness.

Expert System: A type of electronic performance support system, normally a decision-making tool, that has been developed in conjunction with an expert on a job or process. It is designed to help the employee make correct decisions concerning particular tasks related to the job. It is the precursor to an active performance support system.

Facilitator: An individual who is responsible for helping trainees to learn, not by presenting information, but by listening, asking questions, providing ideas, suggesting alternatives, and identifying possible resources. Facilitators are found in the classroom and for self-instructional delivery as well, although their responsibilities are usually very different for these delivery systems.

FAQ (see Frequently Asked Questions).

Feedback: Providing learners with information about an action and its result in relation to some criterion of acceptability. Feedback can be positive, negative, or neutral.

Focus Group: A method of data collection using facilitated group discussions with SMEs. The facilitator leads the process, tries to make sure everyone is involved, and collects data for analysis.

Frequently Asked Questions (FAQ): A file with commonly asked questions and their answers, created to help trainees in self-instructional or asynchronous deliveries.

Graphical User Interface (GUI): A process for allowing the user to communicate with computer software through the use of graphic icons instead of words. Graphical user interface has become the preferred method for communication with computers, but can be tricky if the user does not understand what the icons represent. This is a particular problem in a multicultural environment. (Think Apple versus Windows.)

GUI (see Graphical User Interface).

Guided Simulation: A simulation in which learners receive coaching or feedback during the activity.

Handout: Supporting information used by the learner as reference or activity material in a training program. Handouts are often contained in the participant's package.

Hands-On: An activity in which the trainees practice on actual equipment, simulators, or special training aids.

Hyperlinks: A feature in computer-based training that allows you to program places on a screen that, if selected, will "jump" the trainee to a further explanation of a concept, an example of it, or some other information concerning it or a related topic. This allows for the important process of learner control and for enrichment or remedial activities.

ID (see Instructional Design).

ID Software (see Instructional Design Software).

IDL (see Interactive Distance Learning).

Immediate Feedback: Feedback given to learners at the moment they complete an action or provide some form of input, such as answering a question.

Individualized Instruction: A learning design in which each trainee works on materials without regard to what other trainees in the same class or facility are doing. Sometimes the learning is prescriptive, and it is often self-paced.

Instructional Activity: An activity designed to promote learning and transfer of knowledge. A course is typically a series of lessons made up of instructional activities.

Instructional Design (ID): A systematic approach to creating training that meets the needs of the trainees and the organization while being as effective and efficient as possible.

Instructional Design Software (ID Software): Similar to authoring systems but used before them to guide trainers in making important instructional design decisions for any type of training, but particularly for technology-based training. Instructional design software is usually easier to use than authoring systems, but it is a rare individual who can employ one without some instructional design knowledge. It is sometimes referred to as pre-authoring software.

Instructional Game: A game designed to teach concepts, behaviors, attitudes, or procedures. Can be part of an instructional activity.

Instructional Plan: An intermediate step in program design in which the topic outline is expanded to include sequenced content notations and possible activities.

Instructional Setting: The location and physical characteristics of the place in which a form of instruction takes place. The setting can be in a classroom, laboratory, workplace location, learning center, or any other place in which people receive training.

Instructional Systems Design (ISD): A systematic process of designing learning activities. By following ISD, designers increase the likelihood that their course designs will be appropriate and effective. The most basic form of the ISD model is a five-step process of analysis, design, development, implementation, and evaluation. ISD is often referred to as the ADDIE process as well, using the first letter of each phase in the acronym.

Instructional Technologist: One who is an expert with instructional technologies. This is a dying breed, as no one person can be expert in all the varying technologies available today. Most practitioners consider themselves expert in one or two aspects of technology and work with teams of other experts to create great technology-based training. If you run into someone who claims to be a truly general instructional technologist, watch out for the snake oil.

Instructional Technology: The use of technology (video, computers, CD-ROM, modems, satellites, and so on) to deliver or support training.

Instructor: An individual who provides knowledge or information to learners by directly presenting content and/or directing structured learning experiences.

Instructor-Led Training (ILT): Training that relies on the instructor to present content and create an effective environment for learning.

Interactive Distance Learning (IDL): An interesting term that should simply be redundant, but often is not. It is used mainly to differentiate the old "talking head" tele-courses from more modern techniques in which trainee involvement in the distance-learning process is designed in. It is also used less frequently for the same purpose when differentiating the old "electronic page turners" from newer, more interactive computer-based training approaches. Good instructional design for technology-based training (or any instruction, for that matter) demands plenty of student interaction, so methods in which there is none should not be considered valid training techniques, which is why the term is redundant.

Internet: A global network of networks connecting millions of computer users worldwide.

Intranet: A private network based on the internet standards, but servicing a known organization from behind a secure access point.

Introduction: A major section of a lesson plan designed to establish common ground, capture and hold trainee attention, outline the lesson, point out benefits of the learning, and lead the trainee into the body of the lesson.

ISD (see Instructional Systems Design).

Item Analysis: The process of evaluating test items by determining how well an individual item is answered by examinees, its relative difficulty value, and its correlation with objectives.

JIT (see Just-in-Time).

Job Aid: An easy-to-carry summary of a procedure that the learner can use on the job to aid transfer of learning. It provides guidance on the performance of a specific task or skill. Job aids are used in situations in which it is not feasible or worthwhile to commit the procedure to memory before on-the-job activity.

JTA (Job/Task Analysis): Job analysis and task analysis are often spoken of together (mostly for convenience sake as they are two different processes) as a JTA or job/task analysis.

Just-in-Time (JIT): A method of providing training when it is needed by the trainee rather than when a class is held or a trainer is available.

Learning Center: A designated facility, usually staffed by one or more facilitators, where trainees go to view self-instructional programs.

Learning Content Management System (LCMS): A software application (or set of applications) that manages the creation, storage, use, and reuse of learning content. An LCMS combines the record keeping functionality of a learning management system with the ability to manage the actual content as well. An LCMS may actually include an authoring system for this purpose.

Learning Management System (LMS): Software that automates the administration of training. The LMS registers users, tracks courses in a catalog, records data from learners; and provides reports to management. An LMS is typically designed to handle courses by multiple publishers and providers.

Learning Technology: See "Instructional Technology" and substitute "learning" for "instruction."

Lesson: A portion of a course. Courses may be organized by topics, modules, lessons, or units.

Lesson Plan: A written guide for trainers that provides specific definitions and directions on learning objectives, equipment, instructional media, material requirements, and conduct of the training.

Linear: A programming method characterized by short steps of ordered instruction followed by constructed responses. Also known as *lock step*.

List-Serve: Subscription mailing list on a computer network that automatically sends the user information on a particular topic.

Location: The place a video or still shoot will take place.

Mastery: Meeting all of the specified minimum requirements for a specific performance.

Mastery Learning: A design characteristic in which the trainee is expected to achieve a preset level of mastery for the material to be learned. This mastery level is usually measured through a criterion-referenced evaluation.

Media List: A master list of all media elements included in a program (overheads, print, video, audio, graphics, and animations).

Model: A representation of a process or system that shows the most important aspects of the system in such a way that analysis of the model leads to insights into the system.

Module: A unit of instruction. This term is often used to delineate a self-contained instructional unit that includes one or more learning objectives, appropriate learning materials and methods, and associated criterion-reference measures.

Multimedia Training: A delivery system that incorporates various technology-based instructional methods, such as graphics, text, animation, audio, and video. It is most often delivered on CD-ROM.

Narration: The spoken portion of a video or audio production, especially anything spoken directly to the audience instead of dialogue between the actors.

Navigation: How a user moves through a technology-based training program. Navigation controls are typically a series of buttons or icons.

Needs Assessment: A process used to determine the difference between current and desired states, often related to the development of a training program. A needs assessment may use many data-gathering techniques to discover needs expressed by management, the target audience, or subject-matter experts.

Object-Oriented Design: Creating training as single concepts or small "packets" of information that can be used and reused for many different training needs or programs.

Object-Oriented Learning: A training design in which reusable pieces of content learning, termed *objects*, are created for both a specific training need and for use in other programs.

Objective: A specific statement of what learners will be able to do when they complete a training program or a piece of a program.

Observation: A data-collection technique in which the collector physically observes the subjects' job performance.

Off-the-Shelf: Training produced by an outside agency for use by other organizations. Normally used by organizations when in-house produced training programs would be more costly or take too much time to develop.

OJT (see On-the-Job Training).

On-the-Job Training (OJT): Training in the skills and knowledge needed to perform a job, taking place in the actual work environment.

Online Learning: Often used to mean synchronous e-learning, it is also a delivery method in which the learners communicate with the instructor through discussion boards and chat rooms as they complete preplanned activities and exercises on their own. It can be an excellent methodology for the practice of collaborative learning.

Participant's Package: A set of materials that presents information for use in a learning experience, usually in a classroom setting. This might include general information, procedural and technical use data, or design information, activities, and references.

Passive Performance Support System: Making up the majority of electronic performance support systems, these require the user to recognize the need to stop a task and refer to the system when information is required or a problem that cannot be solved with current knowledge is encountered.

Pass-out: Trainee material, usually in a classroom setting, that is passed out at a specific time in the learning process rather than at the beginning of the program as part of the participant's package.

Performance Checklist: A list of elements that must be correctly performed to determine whether each learner satisfactorily meets the performance standards described in the learning objective.

Performance Evaluation: Evaluations related to the mastery of specific skills rather than knowledge.

Performance Objective: A measurable statement of the behavior that students will be able to demonstrate at the end of the course, the conditions under which they will be demonstrated, and the criteria for acceptable performance.

Post-Test: A test administered after a program or part of a program to assess the level of a learner's knowledge or skill.

Prescriptive Learning: A learning design in which each learner is measured against a set group of skills or competencies and then assigned work based on this measurement. The learning may be individualized, self-paced, or both.

Problem-Based Learning (PBL): An instructional methodology in which the participants (usually in teams) are provided a specific complex problem and asked to solve it as part of the learning experience. The teams work on their own to finalize a solution then meet as a group to discuss not only the solutions but the methods by which they were achieved. In the health care profession this is often called case-based learning as the learners are provide with actual cases to diagnose.

Programmed Instruction: A learning design in which trainees are provided information in small steps, with immediate feedback concerning whether or not the material was learned properly. This allows the trainee to choose the pace at which he or she goes through the material. This concept is often termed *self-instruction*, *self-directed learning*, and *self-paced learning*, although each of these concepts has other definitions as well.

Prototype: An early version of a course developed to test and gain approval of the look and feel and the functionality of the course.

Quiz: A short test to measure achievement on material recently taught or on any small, newly completed unit of work.

Refresher Training: Training that reinforces previous training or helps trainees regain previously acquired skills and knowledge.

Remedial Branch: A technique whereby a wrong answer causes the program to present a new piece of instruction designed to help the trainee master the material, usually from a different point of view.

Script: A list of all spoken lines in a self-instructional course or media production.

SDL (see Self-Directed Learning).

Self-Directed Learning (SDL): Often referred to as individualized instruction or self-managed instruction, in its basic form it is simply training for which there is no instructor present to guide the trainees, who therefore learn on their own. This concept is open to a number of interpretations and more than a little controversy.

Self-Paced: A design characteristic whereby the learner works at his or her own speed to complete the learning assignment.

Self-Quiz: A short assessment, usually self-scored, that allows learners to determine their own understanding or abilities.

Self-Study Guide: A trainee document containing a series of lessons arranged in discrete steps, each of which ends with a self-quiz. It usually includes objectives, subject-matter content, references, review exercises with feedback, and directions to interact with training media, if any.

Sequencing: Arranging the content, objectives, or both into the most appropriate order for effective learning.

Simulation: An instructional technique in which the trainee is presented situations resembling real life that usually involve choices and risks. The players are reinforced for making the right decisions.

Skill: The ability to perform a specific task.

Small-Group Instruction: A training method that places the responsibility for learning on the student through participation in small groups divided out of a larger class.

SME (see Subject-Matter Expert).

SME Review: A review of instruction material done by a subject-matter expert to correct technical errors.

SME-Based Training: Training that is facilitated by an SME who may have, but often does not have, any training experience or formal instruction. The SME is chosen as the facilitator based mainly on his or her being an "expert" on the subject.

Soft Skills: Skills needed to perform on jobs for which outcomes may vary depending on interactions with individuals, such as counseling, supervising, and managing.

Stakeholder: The individual in an organization who requests training or who is responsible for the individuals whom the training will affect.

Storyboard: A document containing sketches of interactions specifying the placement of screen elements (text, graphics, buttons, video windows, and so on) and branching information for CBT, or the scene layout, actions performed, camera angles, and accompanying audio elements for video training.

Subject-Matter Expert (SME): A content expert who works with the instructional designer to ensure the accuracy of information in a course.

Supporting Objective: Objectives that describe something trainees must be able to do prior to accomplishing the terminal or program objective. Also termed *enabling objectives*.

Synchronous: Most often combined with e-learning, *synchronous* refers to instruction using a net-based delivery system in which the instructor and trainees are online at the same time. It is often called *online learning* as well.

Target Audience: The specific audience for whom the program is designed.

Task: A performance, procedure, or behavior. The smallest essential part of a job.

Task Analysis: The process of analyzing a task and breaking it down into its subtasks, skills, and necessary knowledge.

Technology-Based Training (TBT): An overall term for training done with the help of what can be defined as technology. This might include anything from a pencil to a Cray computer, but usually means a device that plugs in, often but not always a computer. Although *technology-based training* is sometimes used synonymously with *computer-based training*, this is often not accurate. Technology-based training is also often considered to be a self-instructional process, but this is not always true either.

Teleconferencing: Meetings held through the use of telephones or satellites. Often considered a form of training, teleconferencing normally lacks any objectives or learning focus. Basically the term is invalid for technology-based training.

Tele-Learning: Simply using the telephone as a training delivery system. It can be an effective and very inexpensive form of distributed training if used for the right reasons and well designed.

Template: A pre-built element that can be used and reused in different programs to speed up the design and development process.

Test: A device or technique used to measure the performance, skill level, or knowledge of a learner on a specific subject matter.

Test Items: Specific items that test trainees' mastery of objectives.

Topical Outline: An outline of the topics to be included in a training program. It may provide course learning objectives; a listing of part, section, and topic titles; and statements of rationale to explain or justify the training.

Trainee Guide: Often used interchangeably with *participant's package* or *workbook*, this term is used at times to indicate a more complex document that guides the trainee through a self-instructional activity.

Training Curriculum: A number of programs or classes that make up all of the training requirements for a job position, department, or entire organization.

Treatment: A written description of a technology-based project, including the story line, the look and feel, how it will work (course flow), and how the course goals will be achieved.

Video Conferencing: Conferencing in which participants both hear and see one another. Usually done over telephone lines.

Video Editing: The process of selecting sections of raw footage and placing them in proper order to create a completed video piece.

Video Still: A single video frame digitized and used as a still image.

Voice-Over: A type of narration in which the speaker's voice is heard without his or her image being displayed on the screen.

WBT (see Web-Based Training).

Web-Based Training (WBT): Instruction delivered over public or private computer networks and displayed by a web browser. Web-based training is usually not downloaded computer-based training, but rather on-demand training stored in a server and accessed across a network. Web-based training can be updated very rapidly. Usually uses a Web browser as the basis for navigation.

White Space: The amount of blank space between areas of print on a piece of printed material.

Workbook (see Self-Study Guide).

Wuzzles: Puzzles consisting of combinations of words, letters, figures, or symbols positioned to create disguised words, phrases, names, places, sayings, etc. Used to energize classrooms and even e-learning experiences.

Index

Page references followed by *fig* indicate an illustrated figure.

A

ABM Mentoring Program Forms and Reports List, 105*fig*

Activities. *See* Classroom activities; Online activities

"Ah Ha" lists, 34

AMB Mentoring Program Objectives, 104*fig*

Asynchronous e-Learning course development: checklists for managing, 70–71; "scope creep" and "neat creep" problems of, 69–70; techniques used for, 54–69

Asynchronous e-Learning courses: advantages of, 53; blended learning applied to, 96–97; blending synchronous course with program of, 97–99; description of, 51–52; development of, 54–71; do's for, 52–53; SDL (Self-directed Learning) applied to, 108–117*fig*. *See also* Classroom course development

Asynchronous e-Learning development techniques: authoring tools and templates as, 68; buying activities as, 62; buying complete off-the-shelf packages as, 60–61; using consultants as, 54–60; customizing vendor off-the-shelf packages as, 61–62; involving stakeholders and end-users as, 68–69; rapid prototyping for, 54, 59; repurposing classroom activities for, 65–67; repurposing video slugs as, 67; scripts and storyboards as, 63–65*fig*, 66*fig*; software tutorial and help functions as, 67–68

Audio recordings, 42

B

Best practices, 2

Beta tests: applications for other delivery formats, 139–141; comparing pilots to, 137; description of, 136; rapid development shortcuts for, 137–139

Blended learning: asynchronous course application of, 96–97; blending asynchronous program/synchronous classroom for, 97–99; description of, 95–96; OJT (on-the-job training) application of, 96; simulations used

About the Author

George M. Piskurich, Ph.D., is a leading authority on instructional design and organizational learning. His design and performance consulting company based in El Paso, Texas, provides consulting services and workshops in instructional design, management development, classroom facilitation, and performance management to clients throughout the country. He specializes in e-learning interventions, performance/training analysis, distance learning, the design and development of self-directed/individualized learning programs for all levels of the organization, telecommuting interventions, and knowledge management. His workshops on instructional design, classroom facilitation skills, self-directed learning, structured mentoring, interactive distance learning, performance management, and telecommuting have been rated as "outstanding" by participants from organizations world-wide.

Dr. Piskurich's recent clients have included major national and multi-national corporations, and government agencies, including Coca-Cola, Wachovia Bank, Baylor Health Care Systems, The U.S. Air Force, The Department of Homeland Security, The Social Security Department, American Family Insurance, Michelin, General Electric, FedEx, Unilever, Merck, Bridgestone/Firestone, Nortel Networks, Sun Microsystems, and Medtronics Inc.

With over twenty years of experience in every phase of learning technology, he has been a classroom instructor in both the public and private sector, designed development systems for managers, developed and instructed training programs ranging from communications theory to computer-based training techniques, and created industrial and health care training departments as a corporate training director and CLO. In his specialty of self-directed learning, Dr. Piskurich has created individualized programs on topics ranging from the biological sciences to instructional and supervisory techniques, using print, slide, video, and computer-based formats.

He holds a Ph.D. in instructional design from The University of Pittsburgh and has been on the faculties of The North Carolina State University, Mercer University, and Peace College.

A sought-after presenter and workshop leader, Dr. Piskurich has been featured at over thirty conferences and symposia, including the International Self-Directed Learning Symposium, the Best of America Conference, Training, and the ISPI and ASTD international conferences. He is an active member of both ISPI and ASTD, where he has held local, regional, and national leadership positions.

Dr. Piskurich is the author and editor of more than fifteen books related to training and development on topics that include instructional technology, performance improvement, e-learning, classroom facilitation, self-directed learning, the basics of training, and telecommuting. His best-selling *Rapid Instructional Design* is now in its second edition. He has authored many journal articles and book chapters on various topics, including customer service, structured mentoring, and corporate downsizing. He has won ASTD's "Instructional Technologist of the Year" award, and ISPI's "Best Use of Instructional Technology in Business" award for his distributed SDL technical skills training design.